Principles
of Union
with Christ

2009. 4月

SJCA

Merry Aze

Principles of Union with Christ

Charles G. Finney

Compiled & Edited by
Louis Gifford Parkhurst, Jr.

BETHANY HOUSE PUBLISHERS
MINNEAPOLIS, MINNESOTA 55438
A Division of Bethany Fellowship, Inc.

Published by Bethany House Publishers
A Division of Bethany Fellowship, Inc.
6820 Auto Club Road, Minneapolis, MN 55438

Printed in the United States of America

Library of Congress Cataloging in Publication Data

Finney, Charles Grandison, 1792–1875.
   Principles of union with Christ.

   First published in 1846 under title: Finney's Lectures on systematic theology.
   Includes index.
   1. Jesus Christ—Person and offices—Meditations.
I. Parkhurst, Louis Gifford, 1946–   . II. Title.
BT201.F56   1985   232   84–24225
ISBN 0–87123–447–5

To My Faithful Friends
in
First Christian Church

CHARLES G. FINNEY was one of America's foremost evangelists. Over half a million people were converted under his ministry in an age that offered neither amplifiers nor mass communications as tools. Harvard Professor Perry Miller affirmed that "Finney led America out of the eighteenth century." As a theologian, he is best known for his *Revival Lectures* and his *Systematic Theology.*

LOUIS GIFFORD PARKHURST, JR., is pastor of First Christian Church of Rochester, Minnesota, and teaches Ethics/Philosophy at Minnesota Bible College. He garnered a B.A. and an M.A. from the University of Oklahoma and an M.Div. degree from Princeton Theological Seminary. He is married and the father of two children.

CONTENTS

INTRODUCTION

Every Christian should know that his past sins are forgiven by grace through the death of God's Son Jesus Christ on the condition of faith in Him. But knowing *only* this, many Christians struggle through this life in almost hopeless despair. They do not believe they will ever have power over the sin in their lives today. They do not know how to move beyond the assurance of forgiveness to victorious living through faith. They make continual confession of their sins, and they ask for God's forgiveness for all the sinful patterns of living which they have not been able to overcome. They wonder how God can keep on forgiving them for their repeated failures or acts of rebellion. They pray, almost weeping, and wonder why these sinful patterns of their past cannot be broken. They do not yet understand the principles of union with Christ.

Yet, Jesus promised that through faith in Him, we can move beyond forgiveness to living a holy life. Each Christian should strive to live a perfect life before God, but only through faith in Jesus Christ can we move toward that goal. Christians can be so transformed that they have the power to overcome any sin, sinful habit, or harmful pattern of living. Especially, God has given Christians the power to overcome and be victorious over every sin which He specifically condemns in the Scriptures. Christians sometimes try to explain sin away, because they have come to believe that they can have no power over certain sins, but God has promised that through faith in Christ not only can every sin be forgiven but every sin or sinful habit can be overcome in this life. If churches and pastors are going to be really helpful today, then they will need to move beyond preaching only the need of forgiveness and acceptance of Jesus, and begin teaching about transformation and holiness in this life, the principles of union with Christ.

After laboring for many years as a revivalist, Charles G. Finney discovered the truth that I have just declared to you. Christians can and must live a holy and transformed life. In 1839, Finney confessed in an open letter to the readers of *The Oberlin Evangelist* that he needed to go beyond working only for the conversion of sinners and begin laboring also for their transformation, or sanctification. He wrote that through his application of the law and the gospel that he had led many to Christ as the Savior of past transgressions. Now, however, he discovered that he must also work with Christians so they could grow beyond their knowledge of sins forgiven to the reality of living a holy life with Jesus Christ as their ever present Savior from the power of sin and temptation in this life. He believed that just as forgiveness was through faith so holy living must also be through faith, and not by a return to the law. He wrote that Christians need to know Jesus Christ in all His relations to their souls through His indwelling Holy Spirit. Just as Christ fulfilled God's promise by His death upon the cross for our sins, so Christ would fulfill His promise of victory over sin in our lives by His new life within us in all His relationships declared by the Scriptures. We need to know Christ as our Sanctifier as well as our Justifier.

Charles Finney prayed through the relationships Christ could have with every Christian, using for his basis the scriptural titles given to Jesus. These periods of prayerful contemplation on the Christ of the Scriptures made a difference in all of his subsequent teaching and labors for revival. He wrote of the spiritual effect upon himself from his prayerful seeking to know Christ according to the nature and character of the various relationships He desires to have with us. Finney wrote: "My soul is filled with wonder, love, and praise, as I am led by the Holy Spirit to discover Christ, sometimes in one and sometimes in another relation, as circumstances and trials develop the need I have of Him. I am more and more 'astonished at the doctrine of the Lord,' and at the Lord himself from year to year. I have come to the conclusion that there is no end to this either in time or in eternity. . . . *I find my wonder more and more excited from one stage of Christian experience to another.* Christ is indeed wonderful, contemplated in every point of view, as God, as God-man, mediator."[1]

In the unabridged English edition of his *Systematic Theology*, Finney lectured on the relationships Jesus should have with the believer as He indwells him. When we know Christ personally, as the Scripture reveals Him, we are able to break the power of sin and temptation through faith in Him. Finney's lectures on our personal relationship with Christ have been compiled and modified as *Principles of Union with Christ*. The lectures have been edited in this devotional format so you can most easily use Finney's method of praying through these relationships and applying them to your life and needs. The brief prayers which I have added to each meditation should be seen only as a start to the prayer and contemplation you should have as you seek for Christ to reveal himself personally to you in the relationship discussed.

May the devotions which follow lead you to know more personally Jesus Christ as Savior from sin and tempta-

---

[1]*Lectures on Systematic Theology* by Charles G. Finney (London: William Tegg and Co., 85 Queen Street, Cheapside, 1851). All references to the *Systematic Theology* in this book are to the 1851 edition.

tion. The Appendix includes other titles for Jesus which you can find in the Scriptures. Seek to know more of Jesus and live your life to the praise of His glory.

For the sake of His Kingdom,

L. G. Parkhurst, Jr.
Christian Life Study Center
P.O. Box 7024
Rochester, Minnesota 55903
October 14, 1984

1

JESUS MY KING

*"Blessed is the king who comes in the name of the Lord!
Peace in heaven and glory in the highest!"* (Luke 19:38).

Jesus comes as King to those of us who believe in Him.
He comes in to set up His government and write His law
within our hearts. He comes to establish His kingdom
within us, and to sway His sceptre over our whole being
and personality. He must be spiritually revealed and received by us personally as our great and glorious King.

We need Him to reveal himself to our souls as the one
upon whose shoulders rests the government of the universe. Jesus is the King! He governs this world for the
protection, discipline, and benefit of all believers in Him.
This revelation of Jesus as King has a powerful sin-subduing tendency in the hearts of those who honor Him as
their King. We will tend to live a more humble and obedient life for our King when we know that all events are
directly or indirectly controlled by Him. We praise Him
knowing that absolutely all things are designed for and
will surely result in our good.[1] These considerations, when

---

[1]See especially Finney's sermon on this in *Principles of Victory*, "All
Things for Good to Those That Love God," pp. 128–136.

revealed to our souls and made living realities by the Holy Spirit, kill selfishness and confirm the love of God in us.

Jesus Christ, who has all power and authority in heaven and on earth, needs to be revealed to our souls, and received by faith, so that He may dwell in and rule over us. We need to see and feel our weakness, our need of protection and defense, and our need of being watched over by Him. We need to see the infinite power of Christ our King for our needs to contend with the power of our spiritual enemies. We need to consider our troubles, our dangers, and our certain ruin without the Almighty One to interpose in our behalf. The soul needs to truly and deeply know itself; and then to be inspired with confidence by a revelation of Christ as God, the Almighty God, and the King who possesses absolute and infinite power. Christ must be presented to our very souls, and we must accept Him and His strength in all our needs for power.

Oh, how infinitely blind we are to the fullness and glory of Christ if we do not know Christ in His power and ourselves in our weaknesses, as revealed to us personally by the Holy Spirit. When we are led by the Holy Spirit to look down into the abyss of our own emptiness—to behold the horrible pit and miry clay of our own sinful habits, which are fleshly, worldly, and devilish entanglements—when we see in the light of God that our emptiness and necessities are infinite; then, and not till then, are we prepared to wholly cast off our selfish self and put on Christ as Lord and King. The glory and fullness of Christ are not revealed to our souls until we discover our need of Him. But when our selfish self is fully revealed in all its loathsomeness and helplessness, when hope is utterly extinct respecting every kind and degree of help in ourselves, and when Christ the King, the all and in all, is revealed to the soul as its all-sufficient portion and salvation; then, and not till then, does the soul know its salvation. This knowledge is the indispensable condition of appropriating faith, or that act of receiving Christ, or that committal of all to Him, that takes Christ home to dwell in the heart of faith, and to preside over all its states and actions. Oh, such a knowledge and such a reception and putting on of Christ is blessed. Happy is he who knows Christ by his own personal experience as King of kings and Lord of lords.

It is indispensable to a steady and implicit faith that the soul should have a spiritual apprehension of what is implied when Christ said that all power was delivered unto Him. His great commission to us was: *"All authority in heaven and on earth has been given to me.* Therefore go and make disciples of all nations, baptizing them in the name of the Father and of the Son and of the Holy Spirit, and teaching them to obey everything I have commanded you. *And surely I will be with you always, to the very end of the age"* (Matt. 28:18b–20, author's emphasis). This great commission included great and precious promises. The ability of Christ to do all, and even exceedingly abundantly above all that we ask or think, is what the soul needs to see clearly in the spiritual sense. We are not to comprehend that Christ is King merely as a theory or as a proposition, but we are to see the true spiritual importance of His lordship in the totality of our lives. This is equally true of all that is said in the Bible about Christ in all of His offices and relationships. It is one thing for you to theorize and speculate and offer opinions about Christ, and an infinitely different thing for you to know Him personally as He is revealed by the Holy Spirit to your heart and mind. When Christ is fully revealed to your soul by the Comforter, you will never again doubt the attainability and reality of personal holiness and entire sanctification in this life.[2]

PRAYER

Come, Holy Comforter, and minister personally to my soul. Show me all the relationships that Jesus Christ wants

---

[2]*Systematic Theology*, pp. 637, 638, 640, 641, 642.

to have and can have with me if I would but open my life completely to Him. Work your gracious will in my heart and mind, because I truly want Jesus Christ to rule in my life and be my one and only Sovereign King. Bring your testimony to my spirit and teach me that He has in reality power and authority over all. Especially impress upon my soul that through Christ the King, I can overcome all sinful habits and temptations in this life for the sake of His glory and the spread of His victorious kingdom. Amen.

2

JESUS MY SAVIOR

*"She will give birth to a son, and you are to give him
the name Jesus, because he will save his people from their
sins"* (Matt. 1:21).

Jesus Christ was born to save us from our sins. As the
prophet foretold, "On that day a fountain will be opened
to the house of David and the inhabitants of Jerusalem,
to cleanse them from sin and impurity" (Zech. 13:1). Jesus
Christ, let it be ever remembered, and spiritually understood and embraced, is not only a justifying Savior, but
also a purifying Savior. His name is Jesus, because He
saves His people from their sins.

As *Jesus,* therefore, He must be spiritually known and
embraced. *Jesus, Savior!* He is called Jesus, or Savior, we
are informed, because He saves His people not only from
hell, but also from their sins. *He saves from hell only upon
condition of His saving from sin.* You have no Savior if
you are not saved from sin in your own experience. Of
what use is it to call Jesus Lord and Savior unless He is
really and practically acknowledged as our Lord and as
our Savior from sin? Shall we call Him "Lord, Lord," and
then not do the things which He has told us to do? Shall
we call Him "Savior," and refuse to embrace Him so as to

17

be saved from our sins and the practice of sinful habits and selfishness?

We must know Jesus as the one whose blood cleanses us from all sin. "How much more, then, will the blood of Christ, who through the eternal Spirit offered himself unblemished to God, cleanse our consciences from acts that lead to death, so that we may serve the living God!" (Heb. 9:14). And the Apostle Peter reminds us, "For you know that it was not with perishable things such as silver and gold that you were redeemed from the empty way of life handed down to you from your forefathers, but with the precious blood of Christ, a lamb without blemish or defect" (1 Pet. 1:18, 19). And he has written to us, "who have been chosen according to the foreknowledge of God the Father, through the sanctifying work of the Spirit, for obedience to Jesus Christ and sprinkling by his blood: Grace and peace be yours in abundance" (1 Pet. 1:2). The Apostle John encourages us by writing in praise of Him for our redemption, "To him who loves us and has freed us from our sins by his blood, and has made us to be a kingdom and priests to serve his God and Father—to him be glory and power for ever and ever!" (Rev. 1:5, 6).

When the shedding of Christ's blood is rightly understood and embraced, when His atonement is properly understood and received by faith, it cleanses the soul from all sin. When Jesus Christ is received as one to cleanse us from sin by His blood, we shall know what James B. Taylor meant when he said, "I have been into the fountain, and am clean." You must know by your personal experience what Christ meant when He said, "You are already clean because of the word I have spoken to you" (John 15:3). You must know His love and know that you are washed clean by the shedding of His blood. Ezekiel declared the promise of God regarding the work of His Son, "I will sprinkle clean water on you, and you will be clean; I will cleanse you from all your impurities and from all your idols. I will give you a new heart and put a new spirit in you; I will remove from you your heart of stone and give you a heart of flesh. And I will put my Spirit in you and move you to follow my decrees and be careful to keep my laws" (Ezek. 36:25–27). It is of foremost importance that language like this, relating to our being cleansed from sin by Christ, should be unfolded to our souls by the Holy Spirit, and embraced by faith, and Christ truly revealed in this relationship. Nothing but this can save us from sin. This will fully and effectually do the work of sanctification in our souls. It will cleanse us from all sin. It will cleanse us from all our filthiness, and from all our idols. It will make us *clean*.

We need to know and appropriate Christ, *our* King and Savior, as dying for *our sins*. It is the work of the Holy Spirit to reveal His death in relation to our individual sins, and as related to our sins as individuals. The soul needs to grasp Christ as crucified *for us*. It is one thing for us to regard the death of Christ merely as the death of a martyr, and an infinitely different thing, as everyone who has had the experience knows, to apprehend His death as a real and authentic vicarious sacrifice *for our sins*. We must know personally that He died as a true substitute for *our* death. We need to recognize Christ as suffering on the cross personally for us, or as our personal substitute. We need to be able to say, "That sacrifice of my God and King was for me! That suffering and that death were for my sins! That blessed Lamb was slain for me!" When we fully and completely realize and appropriate Christ the King and dying Savior, He can kill the practice of sin within us. If knowing Christ in His dying love will not subdue our rebellion against His kingdom, what can?[1]

PRAYER

Lord Jesus, am I so hard of heart that I cannot weep when I think of your dying love for me? Am I so hardened

---

[1] *Systematic Theology*, pp. 673, 674, 639.

in sin and rebellion that I cannot bow willingly and humbly beneath your sceptre? Teach me from your Word and fill me with your Spirit so I can joyfully obey your decrees out of a heart of love. I have one desire, and that is to glorify you. You have done all for me, and I rejoice in your salvation. Help me now to share the Good News of you and your deeds that many might fall down and worship you, renounce their sins, and glorify you forever. Amen.

3

JESUS MY GOD

"For to us a child is born, to us a son is given, and the government will be on his shoulders. And he will be called Wonderful Counselor, Mighty God, Everlasting Father, Prince of Peace. Of the increase of his government and peace there will be no end" (Isa. 9:6, 7).

Isaiah said the Messiah King would be called *Mighty God.* When Jesus Christ stood spiritually revealed to Thomas, he exclaimed, "My Lord and my God!" It was not merely what Christ said to Thomas on that occasion in the Upper Room that caused him to utter the exclamation. Thomas saw indeed that Christ was raised from the dead, but so was Lazarus. The mere fact, therefore, that Christ stood before him as one raised from the dead could not have been conclusive proof that He was God. No doubt the Holy Spirit revealed to Thomas, at the moment of Jesus' personal appearance to him, the divinity of Christ, just as the saints in all ages have had Him revealed to them as the Mighty God. I have long been convinced that it is in vain, so far as any spiritual benefit is concerned, to attempt to convince Unitarians of the proper divinity of Christ. The Scriptures are as plain as they can be upon this subject, and yet it is true that no one can say that

Jesus is Lord but by the Holy Spirit. As I have said in substance often, *the personal revelation of Christ to the inward person by the Holy Spirit is a condition of His being known as the "Mighty God." What is Christ to anyone who does not know Him as God? To any such person, He cannot be a Savior. It is impossible for a person to intelligently and without idolatry commit himself to Jesus as a Savior unless he also knows that He is the true God.* You cannot innocently pray to Jesus nor worship Him, nor commit the soul to His keeping and protection, until you know Him as the Mighty God. To be orthodox merely in theory, or in opinion, is nothing to the purpose of salvation. You must know Christ as God—must believe in or receive Him as God. To receive Him as anything or anyone less than God is *infinitely different* from coming to Him and submitting to Him as the true, living, and Mighty God.

We cannot help but humble ourselves before Jesus Christ and submit ourselves to Him in loving obedience when we receive Him as the Mighty God who became the Propitiation for our sins. Jesus as Mighty God will bring all things to submission before Him as King, but Jesus as our Propitiation will bring us to willingly fall before Him in love and praise as to a Savior from sin. As the Propitiation for our sins, Jesus offered himself to the Father as a propitiatory sacrifice or offering for our sins. It is not spiritually healthy for us to comprehend the mercy of God without regarding the conditions for the exercise of God's mercy. We must be impressed with the sense of the justice and holiness of God, with the guilt and desert of sin. It does not sufficiently awe us and humble us in the dust to regard God as extending pardon unless we consider the sternness of His justice. God's justice requires us to recognize how serious sin is in the universe, as being worthy of the wrath and curse of God. Conditions must be fulfilled before God can be just in forgiveness. One condition of our forgiveness was the death of God's own Son in the atonement (God's provision for our forgiveness and adoption). It is remarkable, and well worthy of consideration, that those who deny the atonement make sin a comparative trifle, and seem to regard God's benevolence or love as simply good nature, rather than for what it is, "a consuming fire" to all the workers of iniquity. Nothing does or can produce that awe of God, that fear and holy dread of sin, that self-abasing, God-justifying spirit, that a thorough apprehension of the atonement of Christ, our Mighty God and King, will do. Nothing other than an appreciation of the atonement can spawn that spirit of self-renunciation, of cleaving to Christ, of taking refuge in His blood that we must have to be victors over sin and selfishness. Christ must be revealed to us in the relationship of Mighty God and also as our Propitiation. In these two relationships, we must apprehend Him and embrace Him personally. This is a condition of personal holiness and entire sanctification in this life. As Mighty God and Propitiation for our sins, Jesus is the Repairer of the breach, or the one who makes good to the government of God our default. In other words, Jesus, by His obedience unto death, rendered to the public justice of God a full governmental (legal) equivalent for the infliction of the penalty of the law upon us. He humbled himself and died the death of a rebel against His own kingdom that He might forgive us our sins and redeem us from the penalty of eternal death. Should we now offer Him not only our praise, but also our lives in holy living before Him? Because He was willing to die on the cross, because He did die and rise again, when He comes to be our Judge, He will pronounce the sentence of acceptance and award us the victor's crown. Should not we live worthy of His great sacrifice now in this life?[1]

PRAYER

Mighty God, Savior, Lord, all praise and glory and honor are yours for the sacrifice you made that I might have

---

[1]*Systematic Theology*, pp. 675, 676, 638.

life, abundant life, eternal life, peace with you. Create in me a clean heart, O God, and put a right spirit within me. When I think of your work in creation and in history, in judgment and in redemption, your Word and Spirit perform a great work of trust in my life. I turn my life over to you completely, knowing that you made me and died for me that I might have life. I entrust my life to you completely that you might do a work of grace in all my relationships with you and with others, for Christ's sake. Amen.

4

WONDERFUL COUNSELOR

"And he will be called Wonderful Counselor, Mighty God, Everlasting Father, Prince of Peace. Of the increase of his government and peace there will be no end" (Isa. 9:6, 7).

"His name shall be called Wonderful." No inward or audible exclamation is more common to me of late years than the term *wonderful*. When contemplating the nature, the character, the offices, the relations, the salvation of Christ, I find myself often mentally, and frequently audibly, exclaiming, "Wonderful!" My soul is filled with wonder, love, and praise as I am led by the Holy Spirit to discover Christ, sometimes in one and sometimes in another relationship that He has personally with me, as circumstances and trials develop the need I have of Him. I am more and more "astonished at the doctrine of the Lord," and at the Lord himself from year to year. I have come to the conclusion that there is no end to this, either in time or in eternity. He will no doubt through all eternity continue to make revelations of himself to His intelligent creatures that will cause them to exclaim, "Wonderful!" I find my wonder more and more excited from one stage of Christian experience to another. Christ is indeed wonderful, contemplated in every point of view, as God, as man, as God-man, mediator, risen Lord, and Savior. Indeed, I hardly know in which of His many relationships He appears most wonderful, when in that relation He is revealed by the Holy Spirit. All, all is wonderful, when He stands revealed to the soul in any of His relations. The soul needs to be so acquainted with Him as to excite and constantly keep awake its wonder and adoration. Contemplate Christ in any point of view, and the wonder of the soul is excited. Look at any feature of His character, at any department of the plan of salvation, at any part that He takes in the glorious work of our redemption; look steadfastly at Him as He is revealed through the gospel by the Holy Spirit, at any time and place, in any of His works or ways, and the soul will instantly exclaim, "Wonderful!" Yes, He shall be called Wonderful!

To also know Christ as our Wisdom, in the true spiritual sense, is doubtless indispensable to our sanctification. He is our wisdom, in the sense of being the whole of our religion. That is, when separated from Him, we have no spiritual life whatever. He is at the bottom of, or the inducing cause of, all our obedience. This we need to clearly understand. Until the soul clearly understands this, it has learned nothing to the purpose of its helplessness, and of Christ's personal spiritual relationship to us.

If you have made Jesus your wisdom, do you recognize how fitting it is to call Him Counselor? Until He is known and embraced in this relation, it is not natural or possible for the soul to go to Him with implicit confidence in every case of doubt. Almost everybody holds in theory that it is proper and necessary to consult Christ in affairs that concern ourselves and His Church. But it is one thing to hold this as opinion, and quite another to apprehend and embrace Christ in this relationship so as to naturally call Him Counselor when approaching Him in secret. Is it natural for you to turn and consult Him on all occasions and respecting everything which concerns you? Do you consult Him too with implicit confidence in His ability and willingness to give you the direction you need in your daily life? Thoroughly and spiritually to know Christ in this relation as your counselor is undoubtedly a condition of abiding steadfast in Him. Unless you know and duly appreciate your dependence upon Him in this relationship, and unless you renounce relying on your own wisdom, unless you substitute His wisdom for the world's wisdom by laying hold of Christ by faith as the counselor of your soul, you will not walk in His counsel, and consequently you will not abide in His love.

Christ our Wonderful Counselor comes to us also as Prophet and High Priest. We must know and receive Christ as Prophet by the Holy Spirit as a condition of entire sanctification. He must be received as the great teacher of our souls, so that every word of His will be received as God speaking to us. This will render the Bible precious and all its words effective to the sanctification of our souls.

As our High Priest, we need to know Christ. I say we need to know Him in this relation as really ever living and ever sustaining this relation to us, offering up, as it were, by continual offering, His own blood, and himself as a propitiation for our sins; as being entered within the veil, and as ever living to make intercession for us. Much precious instruction is to be gathered from this relation of Christ. We need, perishingly need, to know Christ in this relation, as a condition of a right dependence upon Him. I am very embarrassed because I am not able, in this course of instruction, to give a fuller account of Christ in all these relationships that He would have personally with the believer. We need a distinct revelation of Him in each of these relations in order to have a thorough understanding and clear apprehension of that which is implied in each and all of these relations of Christ.[1]

---

[1] *Systematic Theology*, pp. 674, 675, 643, 644, 645.

PRAYER

Dear Lord Jesus, you are wonderful in all of your relationships with me. Counsel me in my Christian experience as I grow from stage to stage in a deeper personal relationship with you. By your Holy Spirit reveal yourself to me personally, so that these words that describe you would not be just words in theory but a living reality that would change my life, empower me to abide always in you, and rescue me from all sin and temptation for your sake. Amen.

5

PRINCE OF PEACE

"Peace I leave with you; my peace I give you. I do not give to you as the world gives. Do not let your hearts be troubled and do not be afraid" (John 14:27).

We must come to know Christ spiritually as the Prince of Peace. "Peace I leave with you; my peace I give you," said Christ. What is this peace? Who is Christ in the relationship of the Prince of Peace? What is it to possess the peace of Christ—to have the peace of God rule in our hearts? Without the revelation of Christ to us by the Holy Spirit, we have no spiritual apprehension of the meaning of Jesus Christ as our Prince of Peace. Nor can we grasp and appropriate Christ as our personal peace. Whoever knows and has embraced Christ as his peace, and as the Prince of Peace, knows what it is to have the peace of God rule in his heart. But you cannot at all understand the true spiritual import of this language, nor can it be explained to you so that you will apprehend it, unless it is explained to you by the Holy Spirit.[1]

---

[1]Jesus Christ is the Prince of Peace in the Kingdom of God. Finney's sermon "The Kingdom of God in Consciousness" explains how we can have "righteousness, peace, and joy in the Holy Ghost" in our own consciousness: see *Principles of Liberty*, pp. 183–194.

Another "putting on" of Christ and important relation in which we need to know Him is as our Passover. We need to understand that the only reason we have not been, and assuredly will not be, slain for sin is that Christ has sprinkled, as our Paschal Lamb, the lintel and doorposts of our souls with His own shed blood. Therefore, the destroying angel passes by us. There is a most deep and sin-subduing, or rather temptation-subduing spirituality in this relationship of Christ to our souls when revealed by the Holy Spirit. We must apprehend our sins as slaying the Lamb, and apply His blood to our souls by faith—His blood, as being our protection and our only trust. We need to know the security there is in being sprinkled with His blood, and the certain and speedy destruction of all who have not taken refuge under it. We need to know also that it will not do for a moment to venture out from under its protection into the streets lest we be slain there.

Even as we trust in the shed blood of Christ, we need to know that Christ is risen for our justification. He arose and loves to procure our certain acquittal (our complete pardon and acceptance with God). We need to know that He lives—and is our Justification—to break the bondage of legal motives, to slay all selfish fear, to break and destroy the power of temptation. The clearly convinced soul is often tempted to despondency and unbelief, to despair of its own acceptance with God; and it would surely fall into the bondage of fear were it not for the faith in Christ as a risen, living, justifying Savior. In this relationship, we need to understand clearly, and appropriate Christ fully in His completeness, as a condition of abiding in a state of disinterested consecration to God.

We need to have Christ revealed to us as bearing our griefs and carrying our sorrows. The clear discovery of Christ as being made sorrowful for us, and as bending under sorrows and griefs which in justice belonged to us, rather than seeing His atonement as simply a mechanical act to procure our pardon, tends at once to render sin unspeakably odious and Christ infinitely precious to our souls. The idea of Christ as our personal substitute needs to be thoroughly developed in our minds, to be so clearly revealed to us that it becomes an everywhere-present reality to us. We need a revelation of Christ to so completely ravish and engross our affections that we would sooner die at once than sin against Him. Is such a thing impossible? Indeed it is not. The Holy Spirit is able and willing and ready to reveal Him to us in this relationship simply by our asking in faith.

Jesus Christ is the one by whose stripes we are healed. We need to know Him as relieving our pains and sufferings by His own, as preventing our death by His own, as sorrowing that we might eternally rejoice, as grieving that we might be unspeakably and eternally glad, as dying in unspeakable agony that we might die in peace and in unspeakable triumph. Thus Jesus Christ is the Prince of Peace, who has given all, suffered all, and triumphed over all so we could have victory over sin in this life.[2]

PRAYER

Come, Prince of Peace, and set up your government in my life. I willingly ask that you set up your throne within my heart, for you are the Prince who died for me that I might have life. Will you not give me all that I need? Only you will never disappoint me; only you will always offer me a hope that will never fade. Lord Jesus, reveal yourself personally to me in the relationship of the Prince of Peace, and may I come to know you so well as my Savior that I can come to you whenever I begin to be afraid of you or fall into a bondage of legalism in my attempt to live perfect before you, for the sake of your glorious kingdom and its establishment upon this earth. Amen.

[2]*Systematic Theology*, pp. 642, 643, 639, 640.

6

CAPTAIN OF SALVATION

"In bringing many sons to glory, it was fitting that God, for whom and through whom everything exists, should make the author [captain[1]]of their salvation perfect through suffering" (Heb. 2:10).

You must come to know Christ as the captain of your salvation, as the skillful conductor, guide, and captain of your soul in all your conflicts with your spiritual enemies, as the one who is ever at hand to lead you on to victory and make you more than a conqueror in all your conflicts with the world, the flesh, and the devil. How indispensable to a living and efficient faith it is and must be for you to clearly discern by the Holy Spirit this relationship of Christ as the Captain of Salvation, and Captain of the Lord's Host. Without confidence in Christ as our leader and Captain, how shall we put ourselves under His guidance and protection in the hour of conflict? We cannot!

The fact is, when the soul is ignorant of Christ as a captain or leader, it will surely fall in battle. If only the church as a body knew Christ as the captain of the Lord's Host: if only He were truly and spiritually known to the

---

[1]King James Version of the Bible has "captain" for "author."

Church in that relation, no more confusion would be seen in the ranks of God's elect. All would be order, strength, and conquest. The Church would soon go up and take possession of the whole territory that has been promised to Christ. The heathen should soon be given to Him for an inheritance, and the uttermost parts of the world for a possession. Joshua knew Christ as the Captain of the Lord's Host (Josh. 5:13–15). Consequently he had more courage, efficiency, and prowess than all Israel besides. It is so even now! When someone can be found who thoroughly knows, and has embraced and appropriated Christ as Captain of Salvation, that person is a host by himself. He has appropriated the attributes of Christ to himself; therefore, his influence is felt in heaven, and on earth, and in hell.

As Captain of Salvation, Christ is also Captain of Sanctification. I have been amazed at the ignorance of the Church and of the ministry respecting Christ as the author of sanctification. He is not our Sanctifier in the sense that He does something to the soul that enables us to stand and persevere in holiness in our own strength. He does not change the structure of the soul, but He watches over, and works in, the soul to will and to do continually, and thus He becomes our Sanctification. *His influence is not exerted once for all, but constantly. When He is discovered and embraced as the soul's Sanctification, He rules in, and reigns over, the soul in so high a sense that He, as it were, develops his own holiness in us.* He, as it were, swallows us up, so enfolds, if I may so say, our wills and our souls in His, that we are willingly led captive by Him. We will and do as He wills within us. He charms the will into a universal bending to His will. He so establishes His throne in us, and His authority over us, that He subdues us to himself. He becomes our sanctification only insofar as we are revealed to ourselves, and He is revealed to us, and as we receive Him and put Him on. What! Has it come to this? Does the Church doubt and reject the doctrine of entire sanctification in this life? Then it must be that the Church has lost sight of Christ as her Sanctification. Is not Christ perfect in all His relationships with us? Is there not a completeness and fullness in Him? When we have embraced Him, are we not complete in Him? The secret of all this doubting about, and opposition to, the doctrine of entire sanctification is to be found in the fact that Christ is not apprehended and embraced as our sanctification. *The Holy Spirit sanctifies only by revealing Christ to us as our sanctification.* He does not speak of himself, but takes of the things of Christ and shows them to us. Among the most prominent ministers in the Presbyterian church, two have said to me within a few years that they had never heard of Christ as the sanctification of the soul. Oh, how many of the ministry of the present day overlook the true spiritual gospel of Christ!

Jesus Christ sanctifies us by bringing and being Redemption to our souls. He is not merely the Redeemer considered in His governmental relation, but He is a present and personal Redeemer and Redemption. To apprehend and receive Christ in this relation, we need first to recognize ourselves as sold under sin, as being the voluntary but real slaves of lust and appetite. Then we need to come to Christ as our Redeemer, and He will continually deliver us from the power of sin by strengthening and confirming our wills in resisting and overcoming the flesh. Oh, to know Christ personally as the Captain of Salvation and our Sanctification and Redemption![2]

PRAYER

Dear Heavenly Father, I praise your holy name for the full salvation you have given me in your Son Jesus Christ. You have given the immeasurable gift of a full and suffi-

---

[2]*Systematic Theology,* pp. 642, 643, 644.

cient Savior, not only for the next life but also for this one. I do bow before you and honor you as King. I do consecrate myself to serving without question the Captain of my Salvation, the Captain of my soul. Indeed there is nothing more satisfying in my life than knowing that my will is willingly led captive by your Son that He might develop holiness in me so I can be the light in the world that you would have me be, for your sake and the sake of those being called into your glorious kingdom. Amen.

7

HEAD OVER ALL

*"And God placed all things under his feet and ap-
pointed him to be head over everything for the church, which
is his body, the fullness of him who fills everything in every
way"* (Eph. 1:22, 23).

We need Christ revealed to our inner being as "head
over everything for the church." All these different relationships we can have with Christ are of no avail to our
sanctification unless they are directly, inwardly, and personally revealed to us by the Holy Spirit. It is one thing
to have thoughts, ideas, and opinions concerning Christ,
and an entirely different thing to know Christ as He is
revealed by the Holy Spirit.

All the relations of Christ imply corresponding necessities and needs in us. When the Holy Spirit has revealed to us the necessity and need we have and Christ
as exactly suited to fully meet that necessity, and has
urged our acceptance of Him in that relation until we have
appropriated Him by faith, a great work is done. But until
we are thus revealed to ourselves in our needs and necessities, and Christ is thus revealed to us and accepted
by us, nothing more is done than to store our heads with
notions or opinions and theories, while our hearts are be-

coming more and more, at every moment, like an impenatrable stone.

I have often feared that many professed Christians know Christ only after the flesh; that is, they have no other knowledge of Christ than what they obtain by reading and hearing about Him, without any special revelation of Him to the inner being by the Holy Spirit. I do not wonder that such professors and ministers should be totally in the dark upon the subject of entire sanctification in this life. *They regard sanctification as brought about by the formation of holy habits, instead of resulting from the revelation of Christ to the soul in all His fullness and relations, and the soul's renunciation of self and appropriation of Christ in these relations.*

Christ is represented in the Bible as the head of the Church. The Church is represented as His Body. He is to the Church what the head is to the body. The head is the seat of the intellect and the will (the living soul). Consider what the body would be without the head, and you may understand what the Church would be without Christ. But as the Church would be without Christ, so each believer would be without Christ.

We need to have our necessities in this respect clearly revealed to us by the Holy Spirit, and this relation of Christ made plain to our understanding. The utter darkness of the human mind in regard to its own spiritual state and wants, and in regard to the relations and fullness of Christ, is truly amazing. His relations, as mentioned in the Bible, are overlooked almost entirely until our needs are discovered. When these are made known, and we begin to inquire earnestly for a remedy, we need not inquire in vain for Scripture promises: "The righteousness that is by faith says: 'Do not say in your heart, "Who will ascend into heaven?" ' (that is, to bring Christ down) 'or "Who will descend into the deep?" ' (that is, to bring Christ up from the dead). But what does it say? 'The word is near you; it is in your mouth and in your heart,' that is, the word of faith we are proclaiming: That if you confess with your mouth, 'Jesus is Lord,' and believe in your heart that God raised him from the dead, you will be saved. For it is with your heart that you believe and are justified, and it is with your mouth that you confess and are saved. As the Scripture says, 'Everyone who trusts in him will never be put to shame' " (Rom. 10:6–11).[1]

PRAYER

Dear Heavenly Father, I thank you for the trials and troubles that I have had, and I rejoice in all things. I do this not only because you have commanded it, and not only because you have promised that all things will work for my good because I love you, but I praise you because my afflictions remind me of my need of you and in them I turn to your Word and find you revealed to my heart in a marvelous way to meet my every need. I thank you for revealing yourself personally to me in your Son Jesus Christ, and may I with His compassion for others seek to do all I can to reveal Him to all in need of Him, the Head over all. Amen.

---

[1]*Systematic Theology*, pp. 640, 641.

8

JESUS MY TEACHER

"When Jesus had finished saying these things, the crowds were amazed at his teaching, because he taught as one who had authority, and not as their teachers of the law" (Matt. 7:28, 29).

We are under an obligation to believe every truth so far as we can understand or grasp it, but no further. So far as we can comprehend the spiritual truths of the gospel without the Holy Spirit, so far, without His aid, we are bound to believe them. But Christ has taught us that we cannot come to Him unless the Father draws us. This "drawing" means "teaching," for Christ says, "No one can come to me unless the Father who sent me draws him, and I will raise him up at the last day. It is written in the Prophets: 'They will all be taught by God.' Everyone who listens to the Father and learns from him comes to me" (John 6:44, 45). This *listening to the Father* and *learning from Him* is something different from the mere oral or written instructions of Christ and the apostles. Christ assured those to whom He preached, with all the plainness with which He was able, that they could not come to Him unless they were drawn, that is, *taught* of the Father. As the Father teaches by the Holy Spirit, Christ's plain teaching in the passage under consideration is that no man can come to Him except he be specially enlightened by the Holy Spirit.

Paul unequivocally teaches the same thing: "Therefore I tell you that no one who is speaking by the Spirit of God says, 'Jesus be cursed,' and no one can say, 'Jesus is Lord,' except by the Holy Spirit" (1 Cor. 12:3). No one, by merely listening to the teaching of the apostles can so apprehend the true divinity of Christ so as to honestly and with spiritual understanding say that *Jesus is the Lord.* What true Christian does not know the radical difference between being taught of man and of God, between the opinions that we form from reading, hearing, and study, and the clear apprehensions of truths that are communicated by the direct and inward illuminations of the Holy Spirit?

Under the gospel, we are entirely without excuse for not enjoying all the light we need from the Holy Spirit, since He is in the world and has been sent for the very purpose of giving us all the knowledge of ourselves and of Christ which we need. His aid is freely proffered to all, and Christ has assured us that the Father is more willing to give the Holy Spirit to those who ask Him than parents are to give good gifts to their children. All of us under the gospel know this, and all of us have light enough to ask in faith for the Holy Spirit, and of course all of us may know of ourselves and of Christ all that we need to know.[1] We are, therefore, able to know and to embrace Christ as fully and as fast as it is our duty to embrace Him. We are able to know Christ in His governmental and spiritual relationships just as fast as we come into circumstances where we need to know Him in these relations.

The Holy Spirit, if He is not quenched and resisted, will surely reveal Christ in all His relationships to us in

---

[1]See especially the section "Be filled with the Spirit" in *Principles of Prayer*, pp. 77–95.

due time, so that in every temptation a way of escape will be open to enable us to bear it. This is expressly promised: "No temptation has seized you except what is common to man. And God is faithful; he will not let you be tempted beyond what you can bear. But when you are tempted, he will also provide a way out so that you can stand up under it" (1 Cor. 10:13).

We are able to know what God offers to teach us within the margin of our ability. The Holy Spirit offers, upon condition of faith in the express promise of God from the Scriptures, to lead everyone into all truth. Every person is, therefore, under obligation to know and do the whole truth, so far and so fast as it is possible for him to do so, with the light of the Holy Spirit.[2]

PRAYER

O Lord, you have called me to know you, and you have spoken your self-authenticating Word in the Holy Scriptures. You have given many great and precious promises regarding how deeply we can know you in our inner being through the filling of your Spirit. You have promised that your Holy Spirit would enlighten me and draw me into all the truth as fast as I am able, obedient, and open to you. I thank you for these gifts of the Word and the Spirit, and I pray that you would strengthen my intention, which is to know you that I might serve you with a love that fills my heart and mind, for the sake of demonstrating your kingdom, power, and glory. Amen.

---

[2]*Systematic Theology*, pp. 647, 648.

9

JESUS MY FRIEND

"Greater love has no one than this, that one lay down his life for his friends. You are my friends if you do what I command. I no longer call you servants, because a servant does not know his master's business. Instead, I have called you friends, for everything that I learned from my Father I have made known to you" (John 15:13–15).

Jesus Christ wants to be our best Friend. He wants to be our Advocate, to plead our cause with the Father. He is our greatest Friend to be our righteous and all-prevailing Advocate to secure the triumph of our cause at the bar of God. In the relationship of Advocate, He must be embraced as our greatest Friend.

Jesus is our Friend and our Redeemer, to redeem us from the curse of the law and from the power and dominion of sin over our lives. When Jesus died upon the cross, laying down His life for us His friends, He paid the price demanded by public justice for our release.[1] Now He can overcome and break up forever our spiritual bondage, through faith in Him. We must always appreciate this

---

[1]One of the best books on the atonement in light of satisfying public justice is *The Atonement*, by Albert Barnes (Minneapolis: Bethany House Publishers, 1860 reprint, n.d.).

relationship which we can have with our beloved Friend.

Jesus is the only Friend who can be our Justification. As our Friend, He procured our pardon and acceptance with God the Father. To know Him also as our Justification is to embrace Him in this relationship and find peace of mind and conscience. We will not feel the condemnation of the law in our conscience or know its accusations in our hearts when we are faithful and obedient to such a friend as He.

Jesus our Friend is our only Mediator. He stands between the offended justice of God and our guilty souls to bring about a reconciliation between our souls and God. We must know Him and receive Him as a Friend, who is our mediator with God the Father in all our prayers and requests to Him for forgiveness and for empowerment to overcome sin.[2]

We need to know Christ, not merely as King and Master, but also as a friend: "Greater love has no one than this, that one lay down his life for his friends" (John 15:13).

Christ took the utmost pains to inspire us with the most implicit confidence in Him and in His work. Many Christians have not apprehended the condescension of Christ sufficiently to appreciate fully, if not to say at all, His most sincere love for them. They seem afraid to regard Him as a friend, as one whom they may approach on all occasions with the utmost confidence and holy familiarity. Jesus as their Friend takes a lively interest in everything that concerns them. He sympathizes with them in all their trials, and feels more tenderly for them than they do for their nearest earthly friends. Now, imagine yourself having an earthly friend who would love you so much that he would die for you, for a crime which you had committed against him. If you were assured of the strength of his friendship, and if you knew that his ability to help you in

---

[2]See especially *Principles of Prayer*, p. 32.

all circumstances was absolutely unlimited, would you not with great confidence share all your troubles and needs with him? How you would rest in his friendship and protection! How slow even Christians are to apprehend Christ in this relationship of a friend! They stand so much in awe of Him that they fear to take home to their hearts the full importance and reality of this relationship of friend when applied to Christ. Yet Christ takes the greatest pains to inspire us with the fullest confidence in His undying and most exalted friendship.

I have often thought that many professed Christians have never really and spiritually apprehended Christ in this relationship of a friend. This accounts for their depending upon Him so little in times of trial. They do not realize that He feels for and sympathizes with them. They do not apprehend spiritually, as a reality, His deep interest and pity for them. Hence they stand aloof, or approach Him only in words, or at most with deep feeling and desire, but not in the unwavering confidence that they shall receive the things which they ask of Him. But to prevail, they must believe: "But when he asks, he must believe and not doubt, because he who doubts is like a wave of the sea, blown and tossed by the wind. That man should not think he will receive anything from the Lord; he is a double-minded man, unstable in all he does" (James 1:6–8).

The real and deep abiding affection of Christ for us and His undying interest in us personally must come to be a living and an omnipresent reality to our souls to secure our own abiding faith and love in all circumstances. There is, perhaps, no relationship with Christ in which we need more thoroughly to know Him than this.

His relationship to us as friend is admitted in words by almost everybody; yet duly realized and believed by very few. How infinitely strange! Christ has given us high evidence of His love for us, and of His friendship for us;

yet many are slow of heart to believe and realize it. But until this truth is really and spiritually apprehended and embraced, the soul will find it impossible to fly to Him in seasons of trial with implicit confidence in His favor and protection. Really apprehend and embrace Christ as a friend who has laid down His life for you, and would not hesitate to do it again were it needful, and rely upon Him. Our confidence in Him will secure our abiding in Him.[3]

PRAYER

Lord Jesus, I am thankful that you are my friend, and such a friend that you died on the cross and would die again if necessary for me. More than I can ever imagine, you love me with a perfect love as a perfect friend. Impress your great friendship and love for me upon my heart and mind—upon my very spirit and soul—that I might have such trust and faith in you that I will rush to you as Savior in every trial and temptation, knowing that your friendship will encourage my faith. O Lord, help me to be faithful to you, for you are always faithful to me. Help me to be that true friend that you can always trust and rely upon in every situation. Amen.

---

[3]*Systematic Theology*, pp. 638, 670, 671.

10

JESUS MY BROTHER

"Then Jesus said to them, 'Do not be afraid. Go and tell my brothers to go to Galilee; there they will see me' " (Matt. 28:10).

Jesus Christ is to be regarded and embraced in the relation of an Elder Brother by us. In Heb. 2:10–18 we learn: "In bringing many sons to glory, it was fitting that God, for whom and through whom everything exists, should make the author of their salvation perfect through suffering. Both the one who makes men holy and those who are made holy are of the same family. So Jesus is not ashamed to call them brothers. He says, 'I will declare your name to my brothers; in the presence of the congregation I will sing your praises.' And again, 'I will put my trust in him.' And again he says, 'Here am I, and the children God has given me.' Since the children have flesh and blood, he too shared in their humanity so that by his death he might destroy him who holds the power of death—that is, the devil—and free those who all their lives were held in slavery by their fear of death. For surely it is not angels he helps, but Abraham's descendants. For this reason he had to be made like his brothers in every way, in order that he might become a merciful and faithful high priest in service to God, and that he might make atonement for the sins of the people. Because he himself suffered when he was tempted, he is able to help those who are being tempted." As our Brother, He was tempted but He never sinned. He never sinned, but in our behalf He was made sin for us.

We need to apprehend that our Elder Brother was treated as a sinner, and even as the chief of sinners on our account. This is the meaning of Scripture, that Christ on our account was treated as if He were a sinner. He was made sin for us, that is, He was treated as a sinner, or rather as being the Representative, or as it were the embodiment of sin for us. Oh! This the soul needs to see and lay hold of: the Holy Jesus treated as a sinner, and as if all sin were concentrated in Him, on our account! We procured this treatment for Him. He consented to take our place in such a sense as to endure the cross and the curse of the law for us. When we apprehend this, we are ready to die with grief and love. Oh, how infinitely we will loathe ourselves under such knowledge as this! In this relationship, Christ our Elder Brother and Representative must be appropriated by faith.

Scripture teaches that Christ was treated as a sinner that we might be treated as righteous; that we might be made personally righteous by faith in Him: "God made him who had no sin to be sin for us, so that in him we might become the righteousness of God" (2 Cor. 5:21). Through faith, we will be made the righteousness of God that we might be made partakers of God's righteousness, as that righteousness exists and is revealed in Christ. In Him and by Him we may be righteous as God is righteous—perfect as God is perfect (Matt. 5:48). We need to see that His being made sin for us was in order that we might be made the righteousness of God in Him. We need to embrace and lay hold by faith that righteousness of God which is brought home to us in Christ our Brother, through the atonement and indwelling Spirit.

After His resurrection from the dead, "Jesus said, 'Do not hold on to me, for I have not yet returned to the Father. Go instead to my brothers and tell them, "I am returning to my Father and your Father, to my God and your God" ' " (John 20:17).

Christ is not merely a friend, but also a brother. He is a brother possessing the attributes of God. And is it not of great importance that in this relationship we should know and embrace Him? It would seem as if all possible pains were taken by Him to inspire in us the most implicit confidence in Him. He is not ashamed to call us brothers; and shall we refuse or neglect to embrace Him in this relationship, and avail ourselves of all that is implied in it?

I have often thought that many professed Christians really regard the relations of Christ as only existing in name, and not at all in reality and fact. "Am I not a brother?" He says to the desponding and tempted soul. He has said that a brother is made for adversity. He is the firstborn among many brothers, and we are to be heirs with Him, heirs of God, and joint heirs with Him of all the infinite riches of the Godhead. "Oh, fools and slow of heart," not to believe and receive this Brother to our most implicit and eternal confidence. He must be spiritually revealed, apprehended, and embraced in this relation as a condition of our experiencing His true brotherhood.

Do let me inquire whether many Christians do not regard such language as pathetic and touching, but after all, as only a figure of speech, as a pretense, rather than as a serious and infinitely important fact. Is the Father really our Father? Then Christ is our Brother, not in a figurative sense merely, but literally and truly our Brother. My Brother? Ah truly, and a brother made for adversity. O Lord, reveal thyself fully to our souls in this relationship of a brother.[1]

---

[1]*Systematic Theology*, pp. 671, 672, 640.

PRAYER

Lord Jesus, come into my heart, come in today, come in to stay. Lord Jesus, reveal yourself to me as my dearest Brother. I thank you for being my best teacher as a friend, but I also praise you for being my Savior as a brother. May I know you in this deepest of relationships, and may I feel as free to call you Brother as I feel free to call your Father, my Father. Walk with me on the road, leading me in paths of righteousness, and do so, Lord Jesus, as a brother walking beside me, for your Name's sake, Amen.

11

JESUS MY HUSBAND

"I am jealous for you with a godly jealousy. I promised you to one husband, to Christ, so that I might present you as a pure virgin to him" (2 Cor. 11:2).

Another precious and most influential relation of Christ in our sanctification is that of the Bridegroom or Husband of the soul. We as individual souls need to be given in marriage to Christ. We must enter into this sacred relationship personally with our own consent. Mere earthly and outward marriages are nothing but sin unless the hearts are married also. True marriage is of the heart. The outward ceremony is only a public manifestation or profession of the union of marriage of the souls, or hearts, of two people. All marriage may be regarded as typical of that union into which the spiritual soul enters with Christ. This relationship of Christ with us is frequently recognized both in the Old and New Testaments.

The relationship of husband to us is treated by Paul as a great mystery. The seventh and eighth chapters of Romans present a striking illustration of the results of our remaining under the law, on the one hand, and of our being married to the Lord Jesus Christ, on the other hand. The seventh chapter begins: "Do you not know, brothers—

for I am speaking to men who know the law—that the law has authority over a man only as long as he lives? For example, by law a married woman is bound to her husband as long as he is alive, but if her husband dies, she is released from the law of marriage. So then, if she marries another man while her husband is still alive, she is called an adulteress. But if her husband dies, she is released from that law and is not an adulteress, even though she marries another man. So, my brothers, you also died to the law through the body of Christ, that you might belong to another,[1] to him who was raised from the dead, in order that we might bear fruit to God" (Rom. 7:1–4).

The Apostle then proceeds to show the results of these two marriages, or relationships, to us. When married to the law, he says of it: "For when we were controlled by the sinful nature, the sinful passions aroused by the law were at work in our bodies, so that we bore fruit for death" (Rom. 7:5). But when married to Christ, he proceeds to say, "But now, by dying to what once bound us, we have been released from the law so that we serve in the new way of the Spirit, and not in the old way of the written code" (Rom. 7:6).

The remaining part of the seventh chapter is occupied with an account of the soul's bondage while married to the law, of its efforts to please its husband, with its continual failures, deep convictions, selfish efforts, consciousness of failures, and its consequent self-condemnation and despondency. It is perfectly obvious, when the allegory with which the Apostle commences this chapter is considered, that he is portraying a legal experience for the purpose of contrasting it with the experience of one who has attained to the liberty of perfect love.

The eighth chapter of Romans represents the results of our marriage to Christ. We are delivered from our bond-

---

[1]KJV "that ye should be married" for "that you might belong."

age to the law, and from the power of the law of sin: "I see another law at work in the members of my body, waging war against the law of my mind and making me a prisoner of the law of sin at work within my members. . . . Who will rescue me from this body of death? Thanks be to God—through Jesus Christ our Lord!" (Rom. 7:23–25).

When we are married to Christ, we are freed and can bring forth fruit unto God. Christ has succeeded in gaining the affections of the soul. What the law could not do Christ has done, and the righteousness of the law is now fulfilled in the soul.

The representation is as follows: First we are married to the law, and we acknowledge our obligation to obey the law as a husband. The husband requires perfect love to God and man. This love, however, is lacking, because we are selfish. This displeases the husband, and he pronounces death against us if we will not love. We recognize the reasonableness of both the requisition to love and the threatening if we don't, and we resolve full obedience to our husband. But being selfish, the command and the threatening only increases the difficulty. All our efforts are for selfish reasons. Our husband is justly firm and imperative in his demands. As his wife, we tremble, and promise, and resolve to be obedient. But all in vain! Our obedience is only feigned, outward, and not love at all. We become disheartened and give up in despair.

As sentence is about to be executed, Christ appears. He witnesses our dilemma. He reveres and honors and loves our husband, the law. He entirely approves our husband's demands and the course he has taken. Christ condemns us, the wife, in most unqualified terms. Still he pities and loves us with deep benevolence. He will consent to nothing which shall have the appearance of disapproving the claims or the course of our husband, the law. His integrity must be openly acknowledged. Our husband must not be dishonored. But, on the contrary, the law must be magnified and made honorable. Still Christ so pities us, the wife, that He is willing to die as our substitute. This He does. We, the wife, are regarded as dying in and by Him, our substitute. Now, since the death of either of the parties is a dissolution of the marriage covenant, and since we, in the person of our substitute, have died under and to the law, our husband, we are now at liberty to marry again.

Then Christ rises from the dead. This striking and overpowering manifestation of disinterested benevolence, on the part of Christ, in dying for us, subdues our selfishness and wins our whole heart. Now He proposes marriage, and we consent with our whole being. Now we find the law of selfishness, or of self-gratification, broken, and the righteousness of the law of love fulfilled in our hearts. Our last husband requires just what the first required, but having won our whole heart, we no longer need to resolve to love, for love is as natural and spontaneous as our breath. Before, the seventh chapter of Romans was the language of our complaint. Now, the language of the eighth chapter is of our triumph. Before, we found ourselves unable to meet the demands of our husband, and equally unable to satisfy our own conscience. Now, we find it easy to obey our husband, and His commandments are not grievous, although they are identical with those of the first husband.

This allegory of the Apostle is not a mere rhetorical flourish. It represents reality, and one of the most important and glorious realities in existence, namely, the real spiritual union of our souls to Christ, and the blessed results of this union, the bringing forth of fruit unto God. This union is, as the Apostle says, a great mystery; nevertheless, it is a glorious reality. "He who unites himself with the Lord is one with him in spirit" (1 Cor. 6:17).

Now until we know what it is to be married to the law, and are able to adopt the language of the seventh of Romans, we are not prepared to see, and appreciate, and be properly affected by, the death and the love of Christ. Great multitudes rest in this first marriage, and do not consent to die and rise again in Christ. They are not married to Christ, and do not know that there is such a thing, and expect to live and die in this bondage, crying out, "What a wretched man I am!" (Rom. 7:24). They need to die and rise again in Christ to a new life, founded in and growing out of a new relationship to Christ. Christ becomes our living head or husband, our surety, our life. He gains and retains our deepest affection, thus writing His law in the heart, and engraving it in the inward parts.

But not only must we know what it is to be married to the law, with its consequent slavery and death, we ourselves must also enter into the marriage relationship with the risen, living Christ. This must not be a theory, an opinion, a tenet; nor must it be an imagination, a mysticism, a notion, a dream. It must be a living, personal, real entering into a personal and living union with Christ, a most entire and universal giving of our self to Him, and a receiving Him in the relation of spiritual husband and head. The Spirit of Christ and our spirit must embrace each other and enter into an everlasting covenant with each other. There must be a mutual giving of selves, and a receiving of each other, a blending of spirits, in such a sense as is intended by Paul in the passage already quoted: "He who unites himself with the Lord is one with him in spirit" (1 Cor. 6:17).

My brother, my sister, do you understand this? Do you know what both these marriages are, with their diverse results? If you do not, make no longer pretense to being sanctified, for you are still in the gall of bitterness and in the bond of iniquity. Escape for your life![2]

---

[2]*Systematic Theology*, pp. 653–655. See also "Legal Experience" and "Christ the Husband of the Church" in *Principles of Victory*, pp. 87–108.

PRAYER

*Lord Jesus, I praise you for dying in my behalf, and
then taking me to yourself as a bride without spot or blemish, in spite of my sin and rebellion against your Father!
Oh, how I love you as the perfect Husband—you do all for
me each day, empowering me with a love within that enables me to obey you in all things from a heart and mind
of true love and devotion for you, your Father, and your
holy law. May I continually grow in a deeper relationship
with you that all I do might be to the praise of your glory
and bring forth fruit for God. Amen.*

12

BREAD AND WATER OF LIFE

"Jesus said to them, 'I tell you the truth, it is not Moses who has given you the bread from heaven, but it is my Father who gives you the true bread from heaven. For the bread of God is he who comes down from heaven and gives life to the world. . . . I am the bread of life. He who comes to me will never go hungry, and he who believes in me will never be thirsty'" (John 6:32–35).

We need to know ourselves as starving souls and Christ as "the bread of life," as the true bread from heaven. We need to know spiritually and experientially what it is to "eat of his flesh, and to drink of his blood," to receive Him as the bread of life, to appreciate Him and appropriate Him as the nourishment of our souls as we appropriate bread, by digestion, to the nourishment of our bodies. This is mysticism to the carnal Christian. But to the truly spiritually-minded, "If a man eats of this bread, he will live forever" (John 6:51). To hear Christ talk of eating His flesh and of drinking His blood was a great stumbling block to the carnal Jews, as it now is to carnal professing Christians. Nevertheless, this is a glorious truth, that Christ is the constant sustenance of the spiritual life, as truly and as literally as food is the sustenance of the body.

But the soul will never eat this bread until it has ceased to attempt to fill itself with husks of its own doings, or with any provision this world can furnish. Do you know, Christian, what it is to eat of this bread? If so, then you shall never die.

Christ also needs to be revealed to the soul as the fountain of the water of life. "If a man is thirsty, let him come to me and drink. Whoever believes in me, as the Scripture has said, streams of living water will flow from within him" (John 7:37, 38). And John also writes of his revelation, "He said to me: 'It is done. I am the Alpha and the Omega, the Beginning and the End. To him who is thirsty I will give to drink without cost from the spring of the water of life. He who overcomes will inherit all this' " (Rev. 21:6, 7). You need to make discoveries that will create such a thirst after God that it cannot be allayed except by a copious drink at the fountain of the water of life. It is indispensable to the establishing of your soul in perfect love that you hunger after the bread of life and thirst for the water of life. Your spirit should pant and struggle after God, and cry out for the *living* God. You should be able to say with truth, "As the deer pants for streams of water, so my soul pants for you, O God. My soul thirsts for God, for the living God. When can I go and meet with God? My tears have been my food day and night" (Ps. 42:1–3).

When this state of mind is induced by the Holy Spirit, so that your longing after perpetual holiness is irrepressible, you are prepared for a revelation of Christ in all those offices and relations that are necessary to secure your establishment in love. Especially are you then prepared to comprehend, appreciate, and appropriate Christ as the bread and water of life, to understand what it is to eat the flesh and drink the blood of the Son of God. You are then in a state to understand what Christ meant when He said, "Blessed are those who hunger and thirst for righteousness, for they will be filled" (Matt. 5:6). You will not only understand what it is to hunger and thirst, but also what it is to be filled: to have the hunger and thirst fully satisfied and the largest desire completely fulfilled. You will then realize in your own experience the truthfulness of the Apostle saying that Christ "is able to do immeasurably more than all we ask or imagine" (Eph. 3:20).

Many stop short of anything even like intense hunger and thirst; others hunger and thirst, but have no idea of the perfect fullness and adaptability of Christ to meet and satisfy the longing of their souls. They therefore do not plead and look for the soul-satisfying revelation of Christ to them personally. They do not expect such divine fullness and satisfaction of soul. They are ignorant of the fullness and perfection of the provisions of the "glorious gospel of the blessed God" (1 Tim. 1:11); consequently, they are not encouraged to hope from the fact that they hunger and thirst after righteousness. If they hunger and thirst after righteousness, the Scripture promises that they shall be filled. But they remain unfed and unfilled, because they do not seek Christ personally and claim His promise in His gospel to us.[1]

PRAYER

Dear Lord, you know that I hunger and thirst after righteousness and for complete victory over sin, and for a Victor to help me overcome every temptation. But, Lord, I confess that I have not expressed my hunger and thirst to you for any intense period of time, for I am too quickly led away to the things of this world which distract me from my real hunger and thirst to those things that will not satisfy. Help me, Lord, with the power and presence of your indwelling Holy Spirit to wait upon you as you would have me wait;

---

[1]*Systematic Theology*, pp. 645, 646.

then fill me with all the fullness of your satisfying presence. And remind me to always eat and drink daily of you, giving me for this day all the bread of your presence that I need for my walk of loving service for you. Amen.

13

HOLY ONE OF GOD

"Simon Peter answered him, 'Lord, to whom shall we go? You have the words of eternal life. We believe and know that you are the Holy One of God' " (John 6:68, 69).

You must know Christ as the Holy One of God, as the true God, and as the Giver of eternal life. But the proper divinity of Christ is never, and never can be, held otherwise than as a mere opinion, a tenet, a speculation, an article of creed, until He is revealed to the inner man by the Holy Spirit. " 'But what about you?' he asked. 'Who do you say I am?' Simon Peter answered, 'You are the Christ, the Son of the living God.' Jesus replied, 'Blessed are you, Simon son of Jonah, for this was not revealed to you by man, but by my Father in heaven' " (Matt. 16:15–17). And Paul has written, "No one can say, 'Jesus is Lord,' except by the Holy Spirit" (1 Cor. 12:3).

Nothing short of an apprehension of Christ, as your personal supreme and living God, can inspire the confidence in Him so essential to your established sanctification and holiness. You can have no understanding of what is intended by His being "eternal life" to you until you spiritually know Him as the true God. When He is spiritually revealed as the true and living God, the way is prepared for the spiritual apprehension of Him as the "eternal life." "For as the Father has life in himself, so he has granted the Son to have life in himself" (John 5:26). "In him was life, and that life was the light of men" (John 1:4). "I give them eternal life, and they shall never perish; no one can snatch them out of my hand. My Father, who has given them to me, is greater than all; no one can snatch them out of my Father's hand. I and the Father are one" (John 10:28–30). "Jesus answered, 'I am the way and the truth and the life. No one comes to the Father except through me'" (John 14:6). "For God so loved the world that he gave his one and only Son, that whoever believes in him shall not perish but have eternal life" (John 3:16). These and similar passages you must spiritually apprehend in order to have a spiritual and personal revelation of them and Him within.

Most professing Christians seem to me to have a wrong idea of the condition upon which the Bible can be made of spiritual use to them. They don't understand that studied as a book, the Bible is only a history of things formerly revealed to men; that it is, in fact, a revelation to no man except upon the condition of its being personally revealed, or revealed to us in particular by the Holy Spirit. The mere fact that we have in the gospel the history of the birth, the life, the death of Christ is no such revelation of Christ to any person as will meet his needs or secure his salvation by itself. Christ and His doctrine, His life and death and resurrection, must be revealed personally by the Holy Spirit to each person to effect his salvation.

So it is with every spiritual truth; without an inward revelation of divine truth to you, divine truth is only an odor of death. *It is in vain to hold to the proper divinity of Christ, as a speculation, a doctrine, a theory, or an opinion, without the revelation of His divine nature and character to you personally by the Holy Spirit.* But if you know Him, and walk with Him as the true God, then you will know that He is all-sufficient and complete as your sanctification.

When we do sin, it is because of our ignorance of Christ. That is, whenever temptation overcomes us, it is because we do not know and avail ourselves of the relation of Christ that would meet our needs. One great need is to correct the developments of our emotional life. Our appetites and passions are enormously developed in their relations to earthly objects. In relation to things of time and sense, our temperaments are greatly developed and alive; but in relation to spiritual truths and objects and eternal realities, we are naturally as dead as stones. *When first converted, if we knew enough of ourselves and of Christ to develop thoroughly and correct the action of our sensibility or feelings, and confirm our wills in a state of entire consecration, we should not fail.* In proportion as the law-work preceding conversion has been thorough, and the revelation of Christ at, or immediately subsequent to, conversion, full and clear, just in that proportion do we witness stability in converts. *In most, if not all, instances, however, the convert is too ignorant of himself, and of course knows too little about Christ, to be established in permanent obedience.* He needs renewed conviction of sin revealed to himself, and Christ revealed to him and formed in him, before he will be steadfast, always abounding in the work of the Lord.

Knowing Christ in all the relationships we have discussed is a condition of our coming into a state of entire consecration to God, or of present sanctification. The soul will abide in this state in the hour of temptation only to the extent that it clings to Christ in such circumstances of trial, and apprehends and appropriates Him by faith in those relationships that meet the present and pressing necessities of the soul. The temptation is the occasion of revealing the necessity, and the Holy Spirit is always ready to reveal Christ in the particular relation suited to the newly-developed necessity. The perception and personal experience of Him in this relation, under these circumstances of trial, is the only means whereby we can remain in the state of entire consecration.[1]

PRAYER

Lord Jesus, I thank you for revealing yourself to me as the Holy One of God, God himself, who as God exists and lives in our midst supported solely by yourself, needing no other. But, Lord, I do need you and cannot live one moment apart from you. I cannot overcome sin and temptation without your loving support and intercession as Victor over all. May your Holy Spirit continue to reveal your historical truths in the Bible to me personally and spiritually that I might know you and myself completely. Amen.

---

[1]*Systematic Theology*, pp. 647, 645.

14

JESUS MY ALL IN ALL

"Here there is no Greek or Jew, circumcised or uncir-cumcised, barbarian, Scythian, slave or free, but Christ is all, and is in all" (Col. 3:11).

We need especially to know Christ as the "all in all." Before you will cease to be overcome by temptation, you must renounce self-dependence in all things. You must, as it were, be self-annihilated. You must cease to think of self as having any ground of dependence other than Jesus in the hour of trial. You must rely on self as nothing in the matter of spiritual life, and on Christ as all. The Psalmist could say, "All my fountains are in you" (Ps. 87:7).

Jesus is the fountain of life. Whatever of life is in us flows directly from Him, as the sap flows from the vine to the branch, or as the rivulet flows from its fountain. The spiritual life that is in us is really Christ's life flowing through us. Our activity, though properly our own, is nevertheless stimulated and directed by His presence and agency within us. So that we can and must say with Paul, "I have been crucified with Christ and I no longer live, but Christ lives in me. The life I live in the body, I live by faith in the Son of God, who loved me and gave himself for me" (Gal. 2:20). It is a great thing for a self-conceited sinner to suffer even in his own view, self-annihilation, as it respects the source of any spiritual obedience to God, or any spiritual good whatever. But this must be before he will learn, on all occasions and in all things, to stand in Christ, to abide in Him as his "ALL."

Oh, the infinite folly and madness of the carnal mind! It would seem that it will always test its own strength before it will depend on Christ. It will look first for resources and help within itself before it will renounce self and make Christ its "all in all." It will commit itself to its own wisdom, righteousness, sanctification, and redemption. In short, there is no office or relation of Christ that will be recognized and embraced until the soul has first come into circumstances to have its needs, in relation to that office of Christ, developed by some trial, and often by some fall under temptation; then, and not until, is Christ clearly and prevailingly revealed by the Holy Spirit so that self is put down and Christ is exalted in the heart. Sin has so becrazed and befooled mankind that when Christ tells them, "Apart from me you can do nothing" (John 15:5), they realize neither what nor how much He means what He says. We will not know how much is really implied in this saying and similar sayings until one trial after another fully develops the appalling fact that without Christ we are nothing, so far as spiritual good is concerned, and that Christ is indeed "all and in all."

It cannot be too distinctly understood, that a particular and personal appropriation of Christ, in such relationships as we find in the Bible, is indispensable to our being rooted and grounded, established and perfected in love. When our utter deficiency and emptiness in any one respect or direction is deeply revealed to us by the Holy Spirit with the corresponding remedy and perfect fullness in Christ, it then remains for us, in this respect and direction, to cast off self and put on Christ. When this is done, when self in that respect and direction is dead, and Christ is risen and lives and reigns in the heart in that relation, all is strong and whole and complete in that department of our life and experience.

For example, suppose we find ourselves constitutionally, or by reason of our relations and circumstances, exposed to certain troubles and temptations that overcome us. Our weakness in this respect we observe in our experience. But upon observing our nakedness and experiencing something of our weakness, we begin by piling resolution upon resolution. We bind ourselves with oaths and promises and covenants, but all in vain. When we purpose to stand, we invariably fall in the presence of temptation. This process of resolving and falling brings us into great discouragement and perplexity until at last the Holy Spirit reveals to us fully that we are attempting to stand and build upon nothing. The utter emptiness and worse than uselessness of our resolutions and self-originated efforts is so clearly seen by us as to annihilate forever self-dependence in this respect.

Now you are prepared for the revelation of Christ to meet this particular want and need. Christ is revealed and apprehended as your substitute, surety, life, and salvation, respecting the particular trouble and weakness of which it has had so full and so humiliating a revelation. Now, if you will utterly and forever cast off and renounce self, and then put on the Lord Jesus Christ, as He is seen to be needed by you to meet whatever problem or temptations you have, then all is complete in Him. This far Christ is reigning within us in place of our self-centered and selfish selves. This far we know what is the power of His resurrection, and are made conformable to His death. This far He will be for us personally all in all in every situation we find ourselves.[1]

---

[1] *Systematic Theology*, pp. 651, 648, 649.

PRAYER

Dear Heavenly Father, I thank you for making Jesus Christ my Savior and also my All in All, that through Him I might find release from every besetting sin and power, to overcome whatever type of sin I have grown to prefer and feel in voluntary bondage to. I thank you that your Word describes so clearly what wrong choices we can make in this world. In this way, we know that we can overcome our bondage to these evil choices through faith in Jesus Christ as He has revealed himself in the Scriptures. May your Holy Spirit continue to press upon me my total need for a total Savior in Jesus Christ my Lord. Amen.

15

THE WORD OF LIFE

"That which was from the beginning, which we have heard, which we have seen with our eyes, which we have looked at and our hands have touched—this we proclaim concerning the Word of life. The life appeared; we have seen it and testify to it, and we proclaim to you the eternal life, which was with the Father and has appeared to us" (1 John 1:1, 2).

We need to know and lay hold upon Christ as the Word of life and as our life. Too much stress cannot be laid upon our personal responsibility to Christ, our individual relationship to Him, our personal interest in Him and obligation to Him. To sanctify our own souls, we need to make every department of religion a personal matter between God and us, to regard every command of the Bible, and every promise, saying, exhortation, threatening—in short, *the whole Bible* as given to us. We must earnestly seek the personal revelation to our own souls of every truth the Bible contains.

No one can too fully understand, or too deeply feel, the necessity of receiving the Bible *with all it contains* as a message sent from heaven to him personally, and to every person, personally. We must earnestly desire or seek the promised Holy Spirit to teach us the true spiritual importance of all the Bible's contents. We must have the Bible made a personal revelation of God to our own hearts by the very Word of Life himself. The Bible must become our own book, as Jesus Christ was the Word of Life to His followers on this earth. We, too, must know Christ for himself. We must know Him in His different relations and offices as revealed in the Scriptures. We must know Him in His blessed and infinite fullness, or we cannot abide in Him; and unless we abide in Christ, He can bring forth none of the fruits of holiness.

Discovering and embracing Christ as our life implies the apprehension of the fact that we of ourselves are dead in trespasses and sins, that we have no life in ourselves, that death has reigned, and will eternally reign in and over us unless Christ becomes our life. Until we know ourselves to be dead and wholly destitute of spiritual life in ourselves, we will never know Christ as our life, or seek Him earnestly as the Word of Life to us. It is not enough for us to hold the opinion that all men are by nature dead in trespasses and sins. It is not enough to hold the opinion that we are, in common with all men, in this condition in and of ourselves. We must see it and know it personally within ourselves. We must know experientially what such language means. It must be made a matter of personal revelation to us, and such is the work of the Holy Spirit in convicting us of sin. We must be made to apprehend fully our own death and Christ as our own life; and we must fully recognize our death and Him as our life by personally renouncing self in this respect, and by laying hold on Him as our own spiritual and eternal life.

Many persons, and strange to say some eminent ministers, are so blinded as to suppose that a person entirely sanctified no longer needs Christ, assuming that such a person has spiritual life in and of himself. They believe there is in the person some foundation or efficient occasion of continued holiness, as if the Holy Spirit had changed his nature, or infused physical holiness or an independent holy principle into him, in such a sense that they have an independent well-spring of holiness within as a part of themselves.

Oh, when will such people cease to offer harmful counsel by words without knowledge upon the infinitely important subject of sanctification! When will such people—when will the Church—understand that Christ is our Sanctification; that we have no life, no holiness, no sanctification, except as we abide in Christ and He in us. Separate from Christ there never is any moral excellence in any person. *Christ does not change the constitution of people in sanctification. He only, by our own consent, gains and keeps the heart. He enthrones himself, with our consent, in the heart, and through the heart extends His influence and His life to all our spiritual being. He lives in us as really and truly as we live in our own bodies. He reigns in our will, and consequently in our emotions, by our own free consent, as really as our wills reign in our bodies.*

Cannot our brethren understand that this is sanctification, and that nothing else is? There is no degree of sanctification that is not to be ascribed to Christ. Entire sanctification is nothing else than the reign of Jesus in the soul. Holiness is nothing more nor less than Christ, the Resurrection and the Life, raising us from spiritual death and reigning in us through righteousness unto eternal life. We must know and embrace Christ as our life! We must abide in Him as a branch abides in the vine! We must not only hold this as an opinion; we must know and act upon it in practice. Oh, when the ministers of reconciliation know and embrace a whole Christ for themselves! When preachers begin to preach Jesus in all His fullness and as present vital power to the Church—when they testify what they have seen, and what their hands have handled of the Word of Life—then, and not till then, will there be a general resurrection of the dry bones of the house of Israel. Amen. Lord, hasten the day![1]

PRAYER

Lord Jesus, you have revealed to me over and over again that I have no spiritual life apart from you. I have fallen when tempted and even sinned with a high hand because I have tried to rely upon my own resolutions, failed, and then given up striving for holiness in my life. Come and indwell me personally. Set up your throne upon my will. I willingly consent to make you Lord over my emotions, thoughts, and actions. I desire holiness that I might fairly represent you to others. Amen.

---

[1]*Systematic Theology*, pp. 649, 650.

16

RESURRECTION AND LIFE

"Jesus said to her, 'I am the resurrection and the life. He who believes in me will live, even though he dies; and whoever lives and believes in me will never die. Do you believe this?' 'Yes, Lord,' she told him, 'I believe that you are the Christ, the Son of God, who was to come into the world' " (John 11:25–27).

You must know Christ as the Resurrection and the Life before you will steadily abide in Him. Through and by Christ, you are raised from spiritual death. Christ, as the resurrection and the life, is raised in your soul. He arises or revives the divine image out of the spiritual death that reigns within us. He is begotten by the Holy Spirit, and born within us. He arises through the death that is within us, and develops His own life within our own being. Will anyone say, "This is a hard teaching. Who can accept it?" (John 6:60). Until we know by our own experience the power of this resurrection within us, we shall never understand "the fellowship of sharing in his sufferings, becoming like him in his death, and so, somehow, to attain to the resurrection from the dead" (Phil. 3:10–11). He raises our will from its fallen state of death in trespasses and sins, or from the state of committal and voluntary enslavement to lust and to self, to a state of conformity to the will of God. Through the intellect, He pours a stream of quickening truth upon the soul. He thus quickens the will into obedience. By making fresh discoveries to us, He strengthens and confirms the will in obedience.

By thus raising, and sustaining, and quickening the will, He rectifies our sinful preferences, and quickens and raises the whole person from the dead, or rather builds up a new and spiritual person upon the death and ruins of the old and carnal self. He raises the same powers and faculties that were dead in trespasses and sins to a spiritual life. He overcomes their death, and inspires them with life. He lives in saints and works in them to will and to do; and they live in Him according to the saying of Christ in His address to His Father: "My prayer is not for them alone. I pray also for those who will believe in me through their message, that all of them may be one, Father, just as you are in me and I am in you. May they also be in us so that the world may believe that you have sent me. I have given them the glory that you gave me, that they may be one as we are one: I in them and you in me. May they be brought to complete unity to let the world know that you sent me and have loved them even as you have loved me" (John 17:20–23).

He does not raise the soul to spiritual life in any such sense that it has life separate from Him for one moment. The spiritual resurrection is a continual one. Christ is the resurrection in the sense that He is the foundation of all our obedience at every moment. He, as it were, raises the soul or the will from the slavery of lust to a conformity to the will of God in every instance and at every moment of its consecration to the will of God.

In reading the Bible, I have often been struck with the fact that the inspired writers were so far ahead of the great mass of professed believers. They write of the relations in which Christ had been spiritually revealed to them. All the names and titles and official relations of Christ must have had great significance for them. They spoke not from theory, of from what men had taught them, but from experience, from what the Holy Spirit had taught them. As the Risen Christ is risen and lives, and is developed in one relation after another in the experience of believers, how striking the writings of inspiration appear!

As our character is developed in experience, and as Christ is revealed, who has not marveled to find in the Bible guideposts and milestones and all the evidences that we could ask or desire that inspired men have gone this way, and have had substantially the same experiences that we have? We are often also struck with the fact that they are so far ahead of us. *At every stage of our progress we feel as if we have a new and improved edition of the Bible. We discover worlds of truth before unnoticed by us— come to know Christ in precious relations in which we have not known of Him before.* And ever, as our real needs are discovered, Christ is seen to be all that we need, just the thing that exactly and fully meets the necessities of our souls. This is indeed "the glorious gospel of the blessed God" (1 Tim. 1:11).[1]

PRAYER

Lord Jesus, I praise you and thank you for being the Resurrection and the Life. Not just in the sense of guaranteeing me a life of eternal bliss in heaven when I die, but in the sense of being the Resurrection Life now in my life. Thank you for subduing my will and transforming my emotional life so that my flesh tries to draw me away from you less and less often in the temptation to return to my former ways. Continue to reveal yourself to me personally in the various relationships you want to have with me as revealed in the Scriptures. Amen.

---

[1]*Systematic Theology*, pp. 651, 652.

17

JESUS MY SHEPHERD

"I am the good shepherd; I know my sheep and my sheep know me—just as the Father knows me and I know the Father—and I lay down my life for the sheep" (John 10:14, 15).

Another interesting and highly important relationship with which Christ sustains His people is Shepherd. This relationship presupposes the helpless and defenseless condition of Christians in this life, and the indispensable necessity of guardianship and protection. Christ was revealed to the Psalmist in this relationship, and when on earth He revealed himself to His disciples in this relationship of the Good Shepherd.

It is not enough, however, for Him to be revealed merely in the letter, or in words, as the Good Shepherd. The real spiritual importance of this relationship, and what is implied in it, needs to be revealed by the Holy Spirit to each Christian personally. The Holy Spirit must inspire that universal trust in the presence, care, and protection of Christ that is often essential to preventing a fall in the hour of temptation. Christ meant all that He said when He professed to be the Good Shepherd that cared for His sheep. He promised not to flee as the hired hand when he sees the wolf; rather, He would lay down His life for His sheep. In this relationship, as in all others, there is a fullness and perfection. If the sheep do thoroughly know and confide in the Shepherd, they will follow Him, will flee to Him for protection in every hour of danger, and will at all times depend upon Him for all things.

Now, all this is received and professed in theory by all who profess to be Christians. And yet how few, comparatively, seem to have had Christ so revealed to them as to have secured the actual embracing of Him in this relation! How few seem to have a continual dependence upon Him for all that is implied in His name, the Good Shepherd!

Now, either this is a vain boast of Christ to call himself the Good Shepherd, or else He may be and ought to be, depended upon; and you have a right to throw yourself upon Him for all that is implied in this name. But this relationship, along with all the other relationships implied by the names of Christ, implies a corresponding need in us. This pressing need we must see and feel, or this relationship with Christ will have no impressive significance. We need in this case, as in all the others, the revelation of the Holy Spirit to make us thoroughly comprehend our dependence upon Christ as the Good Shepherd. The Holy Spirit must reveal Christ in the spirit and fullness of this relationship until we have thoroughly accepted Him in it.

Some persons fall into the mistake of supposing that when their needs and the fullness of Christ have been revealed to their *minds* by the Holy Spirit, the work is done. But unless you actually receive Him, and commit yourself to Him in this relationship, you will soon find to your shame that nothing has really been accomplished toward helping you stand in the hour of temptation. He may be clearly revealed in any of His relations; you may see both your needs and His fullness, and yet forget or neglect to actively and personally receive Him in these relations. You must never forget that receiving Christ personally as the Good Shepherd is indispensable to living a holy life. The revelation of Christ in the Scriptures as the Good Shepherd is designed to secure your acceptance of Him. If it does not do this, you have greatly aggravated your guilt without at all securing any of the benefits of the relationships that Christ wants to have with His sheep.

It is truly amazing to see how common it is, and has been, for ministers to overlook this truth; and of course, neither to practice it themselves nor urge it upon their listeners. Hence, Jesus Christ the Shepherd is not known to the multitudes, and is not in many cases received, even when He is revealed by the Holy Spirit personally. If I am not greatly mistaken, thorough inquiry would show that error upon this subject exists to a most appalling extent. The personal and individual acceptance of Christ in all of the offices and relationships that His various names imply is the foundation of entire sanctification by faith. It seems to be seldom understood or insisted upon by ministers of the present day, and of course little thought of by the Church. The idea of accepting for ourselves a *whole* Savior, of appropriating to our own individual selves all the offices and relations of Jesus, seems to be a rare idea in this age of the Church.

But for what purpose does Jesus Christ provide these relationships? Is the bare understanding of these truths and of Christ in these relations enough, without our own activity being duly excited by the understanding, to lay hold and avail ourselves of His fullness? What folly and madness for the Church to expect to be saved by a neglected Savior! To what purpose is it for the Holy Spirit to make Christ known to us unless we individuals embrace Him and make Him personally our own? If you will but truly and fully comprehend and embrace Christ in this relationship of Good Shepherd, you will never perish, neither will anyone pluck you out of His hand. Knowing Christ in this relationship secures you against following strangers. Knowing Him personally as the Good Shepherd is indispensable to securing you against the wiles of the wolves who would lead you astray and devour you. If we know Him as Shepherd, we shall follow Him and no one else. Let this final thought be well considered in our day.[1]

PRAYER

Lord Jesus, good and loving Shepherd of the sheep who hear your voice and follow you. Speak clearly and loudly to me personally, as I read your Word and look to your Spirit to reveal you to me in the various ways you have chosen to reveal yourself. Guide my thoughts and prayers as I make decisions regarding my future in every area in my life. O Lord, close the gate to the sheepfold if I am about to make the wrong decision regarding anything I am to do or anyplace I believe I should go. Especially protect me from false leaders, the sheep in wolves' clothing, who would lead me out of your protecting care. Make yourself known to me every day, so I might always recognize your voice in time of danger or need and follow you. Amen.

---

[1]*Systematic Theology*, pp. 655–657.

18

GATE TO SALVATION

"I tell you the truth, the man who does not enter the sheep pen by the gate, but climbs in by some other way, is a thief and a robber. The man who enters by the gate is the shepherd of his sheep. The watchman opens the gate for him, and the sheep listen to his voice. . . . I am the gate; whoever enters through me will be saved. He will come in and go out, and find pasture. The thief comes only to steal and kill and destroy; I have come that they may have life, and have it to the full" (John 10:1–3, 9, 10).

Christ is the Gate by and through which you enter the fold and find security and protection among the sheep. This fact needs to be spiritually digested and the Gate needs to be spiritually and personally entered to secure the guardianship of the Good Shepherd. Those who do not spiritually and truly apprehend Christ as the Gate, and who fail to enter by and through Him, and yet hope for salvation, are surely attempting to climb up some other way, and are therefore thieves and robbers. This is a familiar and well-known truth in the mouth, not only of every minister and Christian, but of every Sunday school child. Yet how few really understand and embrace its spiritual importance. All orthodox believers admit that there is no other means or way of access to the fold of God, but how many know and perceive through the personal revelation of the Holy Spirit what Christ means in the very significant words: "I am the gate; whoever enters through me will be saved" (John 10:9). He who truly discovers this Gate, and gains access by it, will surely realize in his own experience the faithfulness of the Good Shepherd, and will go in and out, and find pasture. That is, he will surely be fed, and be led into green pastures and beside the still waters (Ps. 23).

But it is well to inquire what is implied in this relation of Christ.

1. It implies that we are shut out from the protection and favor of God, except as we approach Him through and by Christ.

2. It implies that we need to clearly know and appreciate this fact.

3. We need to discover the Gate, and what is implied both in the Gate itself, and in entering it.

4. Entering the Gate implies the utter renunciation of self, of self-righteousness, self-protection and support, and a putting ourselves entirely under the control and protection of the Shepherd.

5. We need the revelation of the Holy Spirit to make us see clearly the spiritual importance of this revelation, and what is implied in it.

6. When Christ is revealed to us as the Gate, we need to embrace Him, and for ourselves to enter, by and through Him, into the enclosure that everywhere surrounds the children of God.

We need an inward, and not a mere outward revelation of Christ as the Gate. We must have a heart-entering revelation, and not a mere notion, idea, theory, or dream of the imagination. It is really an intelligent act of the mind, as real an entering into the fold or favor of God by and through Christ as to enter the house of God on Sunday by the door. Christ is the Door. When you enter by the Door, you find an infinitely different reception and treatment than those who climb up into the Church on a ladder of mere opinion, a scaling ladder of mere orthodoxy. The people who enter on the ladder of mere opinion are not fed. They find no protection from the Good Shepherd. They do not know the Shepherd, or follow Him, because they have climbed up another way than through Him. They have no confidence in Him, cannot approach Him with boldness, and cannot claim His guardianship and protection. Their knowledge of Christ is but an opinion, a theory, a heartless and fruitless speculation. How many give the saddest proof that they have never entered by the Gate, and consequently have no realization in their own life and experience of the blessed and efficient protection and support of the Good Shepherd.

Here I must insist again upon the necessity of a personal revelation of the titles of Jesus in our relationship to God. Except through Christ the Gate, we are naturally excluded from all access to God and His favor. It is absolutely necessary for you to have a personal revelation, by the Holy Spirit, of Christ as the Gate and of what is implied by meeting God through this Gate. I must insist emphatically upon the absolute necessity of a personal, responsible, active, and full entering in at the Gate, Jesus. We can gain access into the enclosure of the love and favor of God *only* through Him. Let this never for one moment be forgotten or overlooked. You must enter for and by yourself. You must *truly* enter. You must be conscious that you enter. You must be sure that you do not misunderstand what is implied on entering. Only at your peril do you forget or neglect to enter by the only Gate that God has provided.

And here it is important to inquire, have you had this personal and spiritual revelation of Jesus Christ? Have you clearly seen yourself outside the fold, exposed to all the unrelenting cruelty of your spiritual enemies, and shut out forever by your sin from the protection and favor of God? When this has been revealed, have you clearly apprehended Christ as the only Gate to salvation? Have you understood what is implied in His sustaining this relationship with you? And last, but not least, have you entered for yourself, and do you have daily this evidence, that you follow the Good Shepherd and find all you need?[1]

PRAYER

O Lord, sometimes I am tempted to think that you are a harsh and cruel God to make your Son Jesus the only Gate to salvation, but when I remember how you did not spare Him from the cross, that all who believe in Him should not perish, I am overwhelmed by your love. Only His shed blood can cleanse us from our sins, and only His indwelling Spirit can empower us to live holy lives. You allow none to enter heaven with impure hearts and minds. The reasonableness of Christ being the only Gate is only too apparent when I think of your revelation to us of our real need and of your ability to meet it. May I receive more deeply the revelation that I need personally of who you are through Jesus Christ that I might have victory over sin and temptation and be your true and holy representative. Amen.

---

[1]*Systematic Theology*, pp. 657, 658.

19

WAY OF SALVATION

"I am the way and the truth and the life. No one comes to the Father except through me. If you really knew me, you would know my Father as well. From now on, you do know him and have seen him" (John 14:6, 7).

Christ is the Way of Salvation. Observe that He is not a mere teacher of the way, as some vainly imagine and teach. Christ himself is truly "the way." Works are not the way: whether these works are legal or gospel works, whether works of law or works of faith. Works of faith are a condition of salvation, but they are not "the way." Faith is not "the way," but faith is a condition of entering and abiding in this way. Christ himself is "the way." Faith receives Him to reign in the soul, and to be the soul's salvation; but it is Christ himself who is "the way."

You are saved by Christ himself; not by doctrine, not by the Holy Spirit, not by works of any kind, not by faith, or love, or by anything whatever, but by Christ himself. The Holy Spirit reveals and introduces Christ to you, and you to Christ. He takes the things of Christ and shows them to us. But He leaves it to Christ to save us. He urges and induces us to accept Christ, to receive Him by appropriating faith, as He reveals Him to us. But Christ is the way. It is receiving *Him* that saves us. But we must perceive the way; we must enter this way by our own act. We must proceed in this way. We must continue in this way to the end of life, and to all eternity, as the indispensable condition of our salvation. Christ told His disciples, " 'You know the way to the place where I am going.' Thomas said to him, 'Lord, we don't know where you are going, so how can we know the way?' Jesus answered, 'I am the way and the truth and the life' " (John 14:4–6). Christ goes on to so identify himself with the Father as to insist that he who has seen one has also seen the other. Therefore when He says that no man comes to the Father but by Him, we are to understand that no man need expect to find the true God elsewhere than in Him. The visible Christ embodied the true Godhead. He is the way to God because He is the true God, eternal life, and the salvation of the soul.

Many seem to understand Christ the Way as nothing more than a teacher of a system of morality, a system which will save us if we observe it. Others believe this relation only implies that He is the way in the sense of making an atonement, and thus rendering it possible for us to be forgiven. Still others understand this language as implying, not only that Christ made an atonement, and opened up a way of access through His death and mediation to God; but also that He teaches us the great truths essential to our salvation. Now all this, in my apprehension, falls entirely, and I may say *infinitely*, short of the true spiritual meaning of Christ and the true spiritual importance of this relationship. The above is no doubt implied and included in this title of Christ, but this is not all, nor the essential truth intended in Christ's declaration.

He did not say, "I came to open the way, or teach the way, or to call you into the way," *but* "I am the way." Suppose He had merely intended for His instructions to point out the way, or that His death was to open the way, and His teaching to point it out, would He not have said, "What! Have I so long taught you, and have you not understood my doctrine?" Would He not have said, "*I have taught you the way*," instead of saying, "*I am the way*"? The fact is, there is meaning in these words, more profoundly spiritual than His disciples then perceived, and than many now seem capable of understanding. He himself is the Way of Salvation, because He is the salvation of the soul. *He is the way to the Father, because He is in the Father, and the Father in Him.* He is the way to eternal life, because He himself is the very essence and substance of eternal life. When you find Him, you need not look for eternal life, for you have it already.

The questions of both Thomas and Philip, at this time, show how little they really knew of Christ prior to the baptism of the Holy Spirit. Vast multitudes of the professed disciples of the present day seem not to know Christ as the Way. They seem not to have known Christ in this relation as He is revealed by the Holy Spirit. This revelation of Christ as the Way by the Comforter is indispensable to our knowing Him so as to retain our standing in the hour of temptation. We must know, and enter, and walk, and abide in this true and living way for ourselves. It is a living way, not a mere speculation.

Do you, my brother, know Christ by the Holy Spirit as the "living way"? Do you know Christ for yourself, by a personal acquaintance? Or do you know Him only by report, by hearsay, by preaching, by reading, and by study? Do you know Him as in the Father, and the Father in Him? Philip seemed not to have had a spiritual and personal revelation of the proper deity of Christ to his own soul (see John 14:8–14). Have you had this revelation? And when He has been revealed to you as the true and living way, have you by faith personally entered this "way"? Do you abide steadfast in this "way"? Do you know by experience what it is to live, and move, and have your very being in God? Be not deceived: he who does not spiritually discern and enter this way, and abide in it to the end, cannot be saved.

Do see to it, then, that you know the way to be sanctified, to be justified, to be saved. See to it that you do not mistake the way, and betake yourself to some other way. Remember, works are not the way. Faith is not the way. Doctrine is not the way. All these are conditions of salvation, but Christ in His own person is *the Way*. His own life, living in and united to you, is the Way and the only Way of Salvation. You enter this by faith; works of faith result from it and are a condition of abiding in this Way; but the Way is the indwelling, living, personally embraced and appropriated Christ, the true God and the eternal life. Amen, Lord Jesus! The Way is pleasant, and all His paths are peace.[1]

PRAYER

Dear Father, over and over again your Word impresses upon my mind that there is no salvation apart from knowing personally your Son, Jesus Christ. Over and over again, I learn that knowing Him is the same as knowing you, because He is true God, eternal life; and you are in Him as He is in you. Help me to be able to show others that your Son is the only way to salvation. No group, no system, no other person can claim to be the true Way. And help me to know Jesus so well personally that I can lead others beyond His system of teachings to Christ himself. Amen.

---

[1]*Systematic Theology*, pp. 658–660.

20

JESUS MY TRUTH

"If you hold to my teachings, you are really my disciples. Then you will know the truth, and the truth will set you free. . . . I tell you the truth, everyone who sins is a slave to sin. Now a slave has no permanent place in the family, but a son belongs to it forever. So if the Son sets you free, you will be free indeed" (John 8:31, 32, 34–36).

Christ is also "the truth." He said, "I am the way and the truth and the life" (John 14:6). You must apprehend and embrace Him as the truth if you are going to be secure from falling in the hour of trial. In this relation, many have known Christ merely as one who declared the truth, as one who revealed the true God and the way of salvation. This is all they understand by this assertion of Christ, that He is the Truth.

But if this is all, why may not the same with equal truth be said of Moses, and of Paul, and of John? They taught the truth. They revealed the true God, so far as holy lives and true doctrine are concerned; and yet, who ever heard of John, or Paul, or Moses, as being *the* Way or *the* Truth? They taught the way and the truth, but they were neither the Way nor the Truth. Christ claimed to be *the* Truth and *is the Truth*.

What then is truth? We can only answer, "Why, Christ is the Truth!" Whoever knows Christ spiritually knows the Truth! Words are not the Truth. Ideas are not the Truth. Both words and ideas can be true, and they are signs or representatives of the truth. But the truth lives, and has a being and a home in Christ. He is the embodiment and the essence of truth. He is reality. He is substance, not shadow. He is truth revealed. He is elementary, essential, eternal, immutable, necessary, absolute, self-existent, infinite truth. When the Holy Spirit reveals truth, He reveals Christ. When Christ reveals truth, He reveals himself. Philosophers have found it difficult to define truth. Pilate asked Christ, "What is truth?" but did not wait for an answer. The term is doubtless used in a double sense, for all things that exist are only signs, reflections, symbols, representations, or types, of the Author of all things. That is, the universe is only the objective representation of the subjective truth, or is the reflection or reflector of God. It is a mirror that reflects the essential truth, or the true and living God.

But I am aware that no one but the Holy Spirit can convince the mind of the importance of this assertion about Christ. It is full of mystery and darkness, and is a mere figure of speech to one unenlightened by the Holy Spirit, in respect to its true spiritual importance. *The Holy Spirit does not reveal all of the relations of Christ to your soul at once.* Hence, there are many to whom Christ has been revealed in some of His relations, while others are yet veiled from the view. Each distinct name, and office, and relation of Christ, needs to be made the subject of a special and personal revelation to the soul, to meet its needs and necessities and to confirm it in obedience under all circumstances. When Christ is revealed and apprehended as the essential, eternal, immutable truth, and you have embraced Him as such, then you have power for holy living. When your mind recognizes Him as that essential truth, of which all that men call truth is only the reflection, you will find a rock, a resting place, a foundation, a stability, a reality, a power in truth, of which before you had no conception. If this is not intelligible to you, I cannot help it. The Holy Spirit can explain and make you see it; I cannot.

Christ is not truth in the sense of mere doctrine, nor in the sense of a mere teacher of true doctrine, but as the sum and substance or essence of truth. He is that which all truth in doctrine deals with. True doctrine deals with Him, but is not identical with Him. Truth in doctrine is only the sign, or declaration, or representation of truth in essence, of living, absolute, self-existent truth in the God-head. Truth in doctrine, or true doctrine, is a medium through which substantial or essential truth is revealed. But the doctrine or medium is no more identical with truth than light is identical with the objects which it reveals. Truth in doctrine is called light, and is to essential truth what light is to the objects that radiate or reflect it. Light coming from objects is at once the condition of their revelation, and the medium through which they are revealed.

So true doctrine is the condition and the means of knowing Christ the essential truth. All truth in doctrine is only a reflection of Christ, or is a radiation from Christ. When we learn this spiritually, we shall learn to distinguish between doctrine and Him whose radiance it is—to worship Christ as the essential truth, and not the doctrine that reveals Him—to worship God instead of the Bible. We shall then find our way through the shadow to the substance. Many, no doubt, mistake and fall down and worship the doctrine, the preacher, the Bible, the shadow, and do not look for the ineffably glorious substance, of which this bright and sparkling truth is only the sweet and mild reflection or radiation.

Dearly beloved, do not mistake the doctrine for the thing treated of by the doctrine. When you find your intellect enlightened and your emotions quickened by the contemplation of doctrine, do not confuse this with Christ. Look steadily in the direction from which the light emanates until the Holy Spirit enables you to know and grasp the essential truth, and the true light that enlightens every person. Do not mistake a dim reflection of the sun for the sun itself. Do not fall down at a pool and worship the sun dimly reflected from its surface, but lift your eye and see where He stands glorious in essential, and eternal, and ineffable brightness. It is beyond question that multitudes of professed Christians know nothing further than the doctrine of Christ: they never had Christ himself personally revealed or manifested to them. The doctrine of Christ, as taught in the Bible, is intended to direct and draw our minds to Him. You must not remain solely in the doctrine, but receive the living, essential person and substance of Christ. The doctrine makes us acquainted with the facts which are true concerning Christ, and the doctrine presents Him to us for our acceptance. But do not rest in the story of Christ crucified, and risen, and standing at the gate, but open your heart and receive the risen, living and divine Savior as the essential and all-powerful truth to dwell within you forever.[1]

PRAYER

Dear Father, I thank you for your written Word, and I praise you for giving us objectively true facts and propositions about you, reality, and proper relationships. I rest my faith upon you and the revelation you have made of yourself in word, deed, and the person of Jesus Christ. May I continue to immerse myself in your Word, and by your Holy Spirit I pray that you would so impress your Word into my mind, emotions, and will that I might know Jesus

---

[1]*Systematic Theology*, pp. 660–662.

Christ personally not only as Savior and Lord, but in every relationship He can have with me as revealed in the Bible. As I learn more about Jesus personally, may I find victory over all trials and temptations, may I demonstrate His power to effect holy living in every situation. Amen.

21

THE TRUE LIGHT

"Through him all things were made; without him nothing was made that has been made. In him was life, and that life was the light of men. The light shines in the darkness, but the darkness has not understood it" (John 1:3–5).

Jesus Christ is the True Light. John says of Him, "In him was life, and that life was the light of men. The light shines in the darkness, but the darkness has not understood it. There came a man who was sent from God; his name was John. He came as a witness to testify concerning that light, so that through him all men might believe. He himself was not the light. The *true light* that gives light to every man was coming into the world" (John 1:4-9; italics added). Jesus says, "I am the light of the world. Whoever follows me will never walk in darkness, but will have the light of life" (John 8:12). And again, "Walk while you have the light, before darkness overtakes you. The man who walks in the dark does not know where he is going. Put your trust in the light while you have it, so that you may become sons of light" (John 12:35, 36). And again, "When a man believes in me, he does not believe in me only, but in the one who sent me. When he looks at me, he sees the one who sent me. I have come into the world as a light, so that no one who believes in me should stay in darkness" (John 12:44–46).

It is said of Saul, later Paul the Apostle, "As he neared Damascus on his journey, suddenly a light from heaven flashed around him. He fell to the ground and heard a voice say to him, 'Saul, Saul, why do you persecute me?' " (Acts 9:3, 4).[1]

Scripture tells us that when Jesus was transfigured on the mount, "his face shone like the sun, and his clothes became as white as the light" (Matt. 17:2). Paul speaks of Christ as dwelling in light that no man can approach (see 1 Tim. 6:16). Peter says of Jesus and our true relationship with Him, "But you are a chosen people, a royal priesthood, a holy nation, a people belonging to God, that you may declare the praises of him who called you out of darkness into his wonderful light. Once you were not a people, but now you are the people of God; once you had not received mercy, but now you have received mercy" (1 Pet. 2:9, 10). John says, "This is the message we have heard from him and declare to you: God is light; in him there is no darkness at all. If we claim to have fellowship with him yet walk in the darkness, we lie and do not live by the truth. But if we walk in the light, as he is in the light, we have fellowship with one another, and the blood of Jesus, his Son, purifies us from all sin" (1 John 1:5–7). Of the New Jerusalem it is written: "The city does not need the sun or the moon to shine on it, for the glory of God gives it light, and the Lamb is its lamp" (Rev. 21:23).

Light certainly appears to be of two kinds, as every spiritual mind knows: physical and spiritual. Physical, or natural light, reveals or makes manifest physical objects, through the fleshly organ, the eye. Spiritual light is no less real light than physical. In the presence of spiritual

---

[1]For Finney's own experience of light, see his account of his conversion experience, his meeting with Jesus, and his encounter with the light prior to a prayer meeting in *Answers to Prayer*, pp. 14–32.

light, the mind directly sees spiritual truths and objects, as in the presence of material or natural light it distinctly sees material objects. The mind has an eye, or seeing faculty, which uses the material eye and natural light to discern material objects. It is not the eye that sees. It is always the mind that sees. The mind uses the eye merely as an instrument of vision by which it discerns material objects. The eye and the light are conditions of seeing the material universe, but it is always the mind that sees. So the mind directly sees spiritual realities in the presence of spiritual light.

But what is light? What is natural, and what is spiritual light? Are they identical, or are they essentially different? What is the light which often shines upon the pages of the Bible, making its spiritual meaning as manifest to the mind as the letters and the words are? In such seasons, the obscurity is removed from the spirit of the Bible just as really and as visibly as the rising sun would remove the obscurity of midnight from written letters. In one case you perceive letters clearly in the presence of natural light. You have no doubt that you see the letters and words as they are. In the other case, you apprehend the spirit of the Bible just as clearly as you see the letters. You can no more doubt at the time that you see the true spiritual importance of the words than that you see the words themselves. Both the letters and the spirit seem to be set in so strong a light that you know you see both.

Now, what is this light in which the spirit of the Bible is seen? That it is light, every spiritual person knows. He calls it light. He can call it nothing else. At other times the letters are as distinctly visible as before, and yet there is no possibility of discerning the spirit of the Bible. It is known only in letters. We are then left to philologize (study as literature), and philosophize, and theorize, and theologize, and are really in the dark as to the true spiritual importance of the Bible. But when the True Light, who lights every person, shines upon the written Word, we get at once a deeper insight into the real spiritual meaning of the Word than we could have gotten in a lifetime without it. Indeed, the true spiritual meaning and importance of the Bible is hidden from the learning of this world, and revealed to babes who are in the light of Christ.

I have often been afflicted with the fact that true spiritual light is rejected and disdained, and the very idea of its existence is avoided by many men who are wise in the wisdom of this world. But the Bible everywhere abounds with evidence that spiritual light exists, and that its presence is a condition of apprehending the reality and presence of spiritual objects. It has been greatly supposed that the natural sun is the source of natural light. Light is a necessary condition of our beholding the objects of the material universe. But what is the source of spiritual light? The Bible says that Christ is the source, the True Light. But what does this mean? When it is said that He is the True Light, does it mean only that He is the teacher of true doctrine? Or does it mean that He is the light in which the true doctrine is apprehended, or its spiritual meaning and importance understood—that He shines through and upon all spiritual doctrine, and causes its spiritual significance to be apprehended—and that the presence of His light, or in other words *His own presence*, is a condition of any doctrine being spiritually understood? He is no doubt the essential light. Essential, uncreated light is one of the attributes of Christ as God. It is a spiritual attribute of course, but it is an essential and a natural attribute of Christ, and whoever knows Christ after the Spirit, or whoever has a true, spiritual, and personal acquaintance with Christ as God, knows that Christ is light, that His being called Light is not a mere figure of speech; that His wrapping "himself in light as with a garment" (Ps. 104:2; comp. Matt. 17:2); His enlightening the heavenly world with so incredible a light that no man can approach thereunto and live, that the strongest seraphim are unable to look with unveiled face upon His overpowering radiance (see Isa. 6:2). To a spiritual mind these are not mere figures of speech; they are understood by those who walk in the light, the light of Christ, to mean what they say.

I dwell upon this particular relationship of Christ, the True Light, because of the importance of its being understood that Christ is the real and true light who alone can cause us to see spiritual things as they are. Without His light we walk in the midst of the most overpowering circumstances without being at all aware of His presence. Like one surrounded by natural darkness, or as one deprived of sight gropes his way and knows not at what he stumbles over, so one deprived of the presence and light of Christ gropes his way and stumbles at he knows not what. To attain to true spiritual illumination, and to continue to walk in this light, is indispensable to entire sanctification.

Oh, that this were understood! Christ must be known as the true and only light of the soul. This must not be held merely as a tenet or creed. It must be understood and spiritually experienced and known. That Christ is in some indeterminate sense the light of the soul and the True Light is generally admitted, just as multitudes of other things are admitted without being at all spiritually and experimentally understood. But this relation or attribute of Christ must be spiritually known by experience as a condition of abiding in Him. This light is come into the world, and if we do not love darkness rather than light, we will know Christ as the True Light of the soul, and will so walk in the light as not to stumble (see especially 1 John 1:5–7 above).

I desire much to amplify upon this relation of Christ, but must forebear, or I shall too much enlarge this course of instruction. I would only endeavor to impress you deeply with the conviction that Christ is Light, and that this is no figure of speech. Rest not, my brother, until you truly and experimentally know Him as Light. Enter yourself daily into His light so that when you come from your prayer closet, your family and friends shall behold your face shining as if it were the face of an angel.[2]

PRAYER

Come, Lord Jesus, shine your light, the True Light, upon my soul. Enlighten my mind and spiritually reveal your written Word to me. Not once or twice, O Lord, but every time I pray and every time I read your Word, for the sake of obeying you in all things and for all people. Amen.

---

[2]*Systematic Theology*, pp. 662–665.

22

CHRIST IN ME

"You, however, are controlled not by the sinful nature but by the Spirit, if the Spirit of God lives in you. And if anyone does not have the Spirit of Christ, he does not belong to Christ. But if Christ is in you, your body is dead because of sin, yet your spirit is alive because of righteousness. And if the Spirit of him who raised Jesus from the dead is living in you, he who raised Christ from the dead will also give life to your mortal bodies through his Spirit, who lives in you" (Rom. 8:9–11).

Another relation which Christ sustains to the believer, and which is indispensable for you to recognize and spiritually apprehend, as a condition of entire sanctification, is that of "Christ in me."

The Apostle Paul says, "Examine yourselves to see whether you are in the faith; test yourselves. Do you not realize that Christ Jesus is in you—unless, of course, you fail the test?" (2 Cor. 13:5). And to the Galatians who were sorely troubled with a false gospel he writes, "My dear children, for whom I am again in the pains of childbirth until Christ is formed in you" (Gal. 4:19). And again, "I have been crucified with Christ and I no longer live, but Christ lives in me. The life I live in the body, I live by faith in the Son of God, who loved me and gave himself for me" (Gal. 2:20).

Now it has often appeared to me that many know Christ only as an outward Christ, as one who lived several hundred years ago, who died, and arose, and ascended on high, and now lives in heaven. They read all this in the Bible, and in a certain sense they believe it. That is, they admit it to be historically true. But do they have Christ risen within them: living within the veil of their own flesh, and there making intercession for them and in them? This is quite another thing. Christ in heaven making intercession is one thing; this is a great and glorious truth. But *Christ in you*; there also living so that "the Spirit helps us in our weakness. We do not know what we ought to pray, but the Spirit himself intercedes for us with groans that words cannot express. And he who searches our hearts knows the mind of the Spirit, because the Spirit intercedes for the saints in accordance with God's will" (Rom. 8:26, 27).

The Spirit that dwells in the saints is frequently in the Bible represented as the Spirit of Christ, and as Christ himself. Therefore, in the passage just quoted from the eighth chapter of Romans, the Apostle Paul represents the Spirit of God that dwells in the saints as the Spirit of Christ, and as Christ himself (see also Rom. 8:9–11). This is common in the Bible. The Spirit of Christ, then, or the real deity of Christ, dwells in the truly spiritual believer. But this fact needs to be spiritually apprehended and kept distinctly and continually in view: *Christ not only in heaven, but Christ within us, as really and truly inhabiting our bodies as we do, as really in us as we are in ourselves. This is the teaching of the Bible and it must be spiritually apprehended by a divine, personal, and inward revelation to secure our abiding in Him.*

Not only do we need the real presence of Christ within us, but we need His manifested presence to sustain us in hours of conflict. Christ may be really present within us as He is without us, without our apprehending His presence. His manifesting himself to us as with us and in us is upon the condition of our faith and obedience in Him. His manifesting himself within us, and thus assuring us of His constant and real presence, confirms and establishes our confidence and obedience. To know Christ after the flesh, or merely historically as an outward Savior, as Jesus, is of no spiritual avail. *We must know Him as an inward Savior, as Jesus risen and reigning in us, as having arisen and established His throne in our hearts, and as having written and established the authority of His law there.* The old man must be dethroned and crucified, Christ must be risen within us and united to us in such a sense that we two are one in spirit; this is the true and only condition and secret of entire sanctification.

Oh, that it were understood! Why, many ministers talk and write about sanctification just as if they supposed it consisted in, and resulted from, a mere self-originated formation of holy habits. What blindness is this in spiritual guides! *True sanctification consists in entire consecration to God; but be it ever remembered, that this consecration is induced and perpetuated by the Spirit of Christ. The fact that Christ is in us needs to be so clearly seen by us as to annihilate the conception of Christ as only afar off in heaven. The soul needs to apprehend this truth so as to turn within, and not look without, for Christ, so that it will naturally seek communion with Him in the closet of the soul, or within, and not let the thoughts go in search of Him without.* Christ promised in the Scriptures to come and take up His abode with His people, to manifest himself unto them, that the Spirit whom He would send (which was His own Spirit, as abundantly appears from the Bible) should abide with them forever, that He should be with them and in them.

Now, all this language needs to be spiritually grasped, and Christ needs to be revealed by His Spirit as being as near and present with us as we are with ourselves, and as infinitely more interested in us than we are in ourselves. This spiritual recognition of Christ present with and in us has an overpowering charm in it. You will rest in Him, live, walk, and have your being in His light, and drink at the fountain of His love. You will drink also of the river of His pleasures. You will enjoy His peace and lean upon His strength.

Many professing Christians do not have Christ formed within them. The Galatian Christians had fallen from Christ. Hence, the Apostle Paul says, "My dear children, for whom I am again in the pains of childbirth until Christ is formed in you" (Gal. 4:19). Have you a spiritual understanding of what this means?[1]

PRAYER

Lord Jesus, I thank you that you know me better than I know myself. I humbly bow before you at the thought that you care more about me than I care about myself. Your love for me is beyond my comprehension, and your abiding in me is more than I can understand. You know my thoughts, understand my struggles, help me wrestle with the emotions that would pull me away from faith and obedience to you. You are not a far-off God to me, but an ever-present help in time of trouble. Please continue to transform my life from within as your indwelling Spirit works with my spirit to conform me fully to the image of God that you created me to be. May I represent you in all my actions and relationships with others. For your Name's sake, amen.

---

[1]*Systematic Theology*, pp. 665–667.

23

JESUS MY STRENGTH

"I love you, O Lord, my strength. The Lord is my rock, my fortress and my deliverer, my God is my rock, in whom I take refuge. He is my shield and the horn of my salvation, my stronghold. I call to the Lord, who is worthy of praise, and I am saved from my enemies" (Ps. 18:1–3).

We must spiritually know Christ as "our strength," as a condition of entire sanctification. Says the Psalmist, "I love you, O Lord, my strength" (Ps. 18:1). And again, "O my Strength, I sing praise to you; you, O God, are my fortress, my loving God" (Ps. 59:17). Jeremiah the prophet says, "O Lord, my strength and my fortress, my refuge in time of distress, to you the nations will come from the ends of the earth and say, 'Our fathers possessed nothing but false gods, worthless idols that did them no good. Do men make their own gods? Yes, but they are not gods!' Therefore I will teach them—this time I will teach them my power and might. Then they will know that my name is the Lord" (Jer. 16:19–21). And to Paul, after he had prayed three times for healing, Jesus said, "My grace is sufficient for you, for my power[1] is made perfect in weakness" (2 Cor. 12:9).

---

[1]"strength" in KJV.

We are commanded to be strong in the Lord and in the power of His might, that is, to appropriate His strength by faith. We are exhorted to take hold on His strength, and doing this is a condition of our making peace with God. That God is in some sense our strength is generally admitted. But I fear it is rare to comprehend the true spiritual sense in which He is our strength. Many take refuge not in His strength by faith, but in the plea that He is their strength, and that they have none of their own, while they continue in sin. But this class of persons neither truly understand nor believe that God is their strength. So it is with all who hold this language and yet live in sin. For them, Jesus my Strength is an opinion or a say-so, but by no means is it a spiritually understood and embraced truth. If the real meaning of this language were spiritually understood and embraced with the heart, you would no more live in sin. You could no more be overcome with temptation while appropriating Christ than God could be overcome.

The conditions of spiritually apprehending Christ as our strength are: (1) The spiritual realization of our own weakness, its nature and degree. (2) The revelation of Christ to us as our strength by the Holy Spirit.

When these revelations are truly made, and self-dependence is, therefore, forever annihilated, you will come to understand wherein your strength lies. You renounce forever your own strength, and rely wholly on the strength of Christ. You do not do this in the antinomian do-nothing, sit-still sense of the term. On the contrary, you actively take hold of Christ's strength, and use it in doing all the will of God. You set about doing every good word and work as one might lean upon the strength of another. You must understand and do this: hold on to and lean upon Christ, as a helpless man would lean upon the arm or shoulder of a strong man to be borne about in some benevolent enterprise. You are not in a state of quietism. This is not a mere opinion, a sentiment, or a fancy. "Jesus my Strength" is, with the sanctified soul, one of the clearest realities in existence; that is, you may lean upon and use the strength of Christ personally. You will know yourself to be constantly and perseveringly active in thus availing yourself of the strength of Christ. You will be conscious of being perfectly weak in yourself, or perfectly emptied of your own strength, and know that Christ's strength is made perfect in your weakness.

This renunciation of your own strength is not a denial of natural ability in any such sense as to virtually charge God with requiring what you are unable to perform. It is a complete recognition of your ability were you disposed to do all that God requires of you, and implies a thorough and honest condemnation of yourself for not using your powers as God requires. But while you recognize your natural liberty or ability, and your consequent obligation to God and your fellowman, you at the same time clearly and spiritually see that you have been too long the slave of lust ever to assert or to maintain your spiritual supremacy over sin or temptation as a master instead of a slave to appetite. You see so clearly and pitifully that your will or heart is so weak in the presence of temptation that there is no hope of maintaining your integrity unsupported by strength from Christ. You renounce forever your dependence upon your own strength, and cast yourself wholly and forever on the strength of Christ. Christ's strength is appropriated only upon condition of a full renunciation of your own strength. And Christ's strength is made perfect in you only in your entire weakness; that is, only in the absence of all dependence on your own strength. Self must be renounced in every respect in which we appropriate Christ. He will not share the throne of the heart with us, nor will He be put on by us, except insofar as we put off ourselves. Lay aside all dependence on yourself in every respect in which you would have Christ. Many reject Christ by depending upon self, and seem not to be aware of their error.

Now, let it be understood and constantly borne in mind that this self-renunciation and taking hold on Christ as our strength is not a mere speculation, an opinion, an article of faith, a profession, but must be one of the most practical realities in the world. It must become to the mind an omnipresent reality, that you shall no more attempt anything in your own strength than a man who could never walk without crutches would attempt to arise and walk without thinking of them. To such a one, his crutches become a part of himself. They are his legs. He as naturally uses them as we do the members of our body. He no more forgets them, or attempts to walk without them, than we attempt to walk without our feet. Now just so it is with one who spiritually understands his dependence on Christ. He knows he can walk, and that he must walk, but he as naturally uses the strength of Christ in all his duties as the lame man uses his crutches. It is as really an omnipresent reality to him that he must lean upon Christ as it is to the lame man that he must lean upon his crutch. He learns on all occasions to keep hold of the strength of Christ, and does not think of doing anything without Him. He knows that he need not attempt anything in his own strength; and that if he should, it will result in failure and disgrace, just as really as the man without feet or legs knows that for him to attempt to walk without his crutch would ensure a fall. This is a great, and, I fear, a rarely learned lesson with professing Christians. Yet how strange that it should be so, since every attempt to walk without Christ has resulted in complete and instantaneous failure. All profess to know their own weakness and their remedy, and yet how few give evidence of knowing either. How few go to Jesus moment-by-moment and exclaim from the heart, "Jesus my Strength!"[2]

---

[2]*Systematic Theology*, pp. 667–669.

PRAYER

"Let the words of my mouth, and the meditation of my heart, be acceptable in thy sight, O Lord, my strength and my redeemer" (Ps. 19:14, KJV). This is my prayer, O Lord. You know my inmost thoughts, and how I try to rely on myself, and how I put "Christian service" ahead of taking the time to hear from you and put on your strength before I do anything. Forgive me for putting what I am going to do for you ahead of first allowing you to do all for me, so that your strength would be manifest in all that I do with reliance upon you in my weakness. Amen.

24

KEEPER OF MY SOUL

"I lift up my eyes to the hills—where does my help come from? My help comes from the Lord, the Maker of heaven and earth. He will not let your foot slip—he who watches[1] over you will not slumber; indeed, he who watches[1] over Israel will neither slumber nor sleep. The Lord watches over you[2]—the Lord is your shade at your right hand; the sun will not harm you by day, nor the moon by night. The Lord will keep you from all harm—he will watch over your life; the Lord will watch over your coming and going both now and forevermore" (Ps. 121).

Christ Jesus is also the "Keeper of my soul." In this relationship He must be revealed to, and embraced by, each soul as a condition of abiding in Christ, or, which is the same thing, as a condition of entire sanctification. Psalm 121, along with a great many other passages of Scripture, represents God as exerting an efficient influence in preserving the soul from falling. This influence He exerts, of course not physically or by compulsion, is and must be a moral influence; that is, an influence entirely

---

[1]"keepeth" (KJV).
[2]"The Lord is thy keeper" (KJV).

consistent with our own free agency. But it is efficient in the sense of being a prevailing influence.

But in this relationship, as in all others, Christ must be apprehended and embraced. You must see and well appreciate your dependence in this respect, and commit yourself to Christ in this relationship of "Keeper of your soul." You must cease from your own works, and from expecting to keep yourself, and commit yourself to Christ and abide in this state of committal. Keeping the soul implies watching over it to guard it against being overcome with temptation. This is exactly what the Christian needs! His enemies are the world, the flesh, and Satan. By these he has been enslaved. To them he has been consecrated. In their presence he is all weakness in himself. He needs a keeper to accompany him, just as a reformed alcoholic sometimes needs one to accompany him and strengthen him in scenes of temptation. The long-established habits of the drunkard render him weak in the presence of his enemy, the intoxicating glass. So the Christian's long-cherished habits of self-indulgence render him all weakness and irresolution if left to himself in the presence of excited appetite or passion. As the alcoholic needs a friend and brother to warn and earnestly protest, to suggest considerations to strengthen his purposes, so the sinner needs the Parakletos, or Comforter, to warn and suggest considerations to sustain his fainting resolution.

This Christ has promised to do; but this, like all the promises, is conditioned upon our appropriating the promise by faith. Let it then be ever borne in mind, that as our keeper, the Lord must be spiritually known, embraced, and depended upon as a condition of entire sanctification. This must not be a mere opinion. It must be a thorough and honest commitment to Christ in this relation.

Brother, do you know what it is to depend on Christ in this relationship so that you as naturally hold fast to Him as a child would cling to the hand or the neck of a father when in the midst of perceived danger? Have you seen your need of a keeper? If so, have you fled to Christ in this relationship of Keeper of your soul? As you have received Christ Jesus the Lord, so walk in Him; that is, abide in Him, and He will abide in you and keep you from falling. The Apostle certifies, or rather assumes, that Christ is able to keep you from falling: "To him who is able to keep you from falling and to present you before his glorious presence without fault and with great joy—to the only God our Savior be glory, majesty, power and authority, through Jesus Christ our Lord, before all ages, now and forevermore! Amen" (Jude 24, 25). Paul also says, "I know whom I have believed, and am convinced that he is able to guard what I have entrusted to him for that day" (2 Tim. 1:12).[3]

PRAYER

Lord Jesus, thank you for keeping me from the degradation of sinful habits. Indeed, were it not for your indwelling presence as Keeper of my soul, I would betray your trust and defame your holy name. Guard me and my every action, that I might honor you with my life in everything I do. May I know from experience, so as to tell others, that you can be trusted to help us overcome every temptation from the flesh, the world, or the devil. Amen.

---

[3]*Systematic Theology*, pp. 669, 670.

25

THE TRUE VINE

"I am the true vine and my Father is the gardener. He cuts off every branch in me that bears no fruit, while every branch that does bear fruit he trims clean so that it will be even more fruitful. You are already clean because of the word I have spoken to you. Remain in me, and I will remain in you. No branch can bear fruit by itself; it must remain in the vine. Neither can you bear fruit unless you remain in me" (John 15:1–4).

Jesus Christ is "the True Vine," and we are the branches. Do we know Him in this relationship, as our parent stalk, as the fountain from whom we receive our moment-by-moment nourishment and life? This union between Christ and our souls is formed by implicit faith in Him. By faith we lean on Him, feed upon Him, and receive a constantly sustaining influence from Him. Jesus makes this clear to us by saying, "I am the vine; you are the branches. If a man remains in me and I in him, he will bear much fruit; apart from me you can do nothing. If anyone does not remain in me, he is like a branch that is thrown away and withers; such branches are picked up, thrown into the fire and burned. If you remain in me and my words remain in you, ask whatever you wish, and it will be given you. This is to my Father's glory, that you bear much fruit, showing yourselves to be my disciples" (John 15:5–8).

Now, it is important for us to understand what it is to be in Christ, in the sense of this passage. It is to be so united to Him as to receive as real and as constant spiritual support and nourishment from Him as the branch does natural nourishment from the vine. "If anyone does not remain in me, he is like a branch that is thrown away and withers" (John 15:6), He says. Now, to be in Him implies such a union as to keep us spiritually alive and fresh. There are many withered professing Christians in the church. They abide not in Christ. Their religion is stale. They can speak of former experiences. They can tell how they once knew Christ, but every spiritual mind can see that they are branches fallen off. They have no fruit. Their leaves are withered. Their bark is dried. They are just fit to be gathered and cast into the fire. Oh, this stale, last year's religion! Why won't professing Christians, who live on an old experience, understand that they are cast-off branches, and that their withered, fruitless, lifeless, loveless, faithless, powerless condition testifies to their faces, and before all people, that they are ready fuel for the flames?

It is also of infinite importance that we should know and spiritually apprehend the conditions of abiding in Christ in the relation of a branch to a vine. We must apprehend our various necessities and His infinite fullness. We must lay hold upon and appropriate all that God's Word has implied in these relations to us, in all our needs as they are revealed to us. Thus we shall abide in Him, and receive all the spiritual nourishment that we need. But unless we are thus taught by the Spirit, and unless we thus believe, we shall not abide in Him, nor He in us. If we do thus abide in Him, He says that we shall bear much fruit. *Much fruit, then, is evidence that we do abide*

*in Him, and fruitlessness is positive evidence that we do
not abide in Him.* "If you remain in me and my words
remain in you, ask whatever you wish, and it will be given
you" (John 15:7). *Great success in prayer, then, is an evidence that we abide in Him.* But a lack of prevailing prayer
is conclusive evidence that we do not abide in Him. *No
man sins while he properly abides in Christ.* For Scripture
assures us, "Therefore, if anyone is in Christ, he is a new
creation; the old has gone, the new has come!" (2 Cor.
5:17).

But let it not be forgotten that abiding in Christ is
conditional. "Remain in me," says Christ. This He requires of us! We cannot begin the relation of a branch to
Christ without our own actively coming to Him, nor can
we remain in Him without our actively, constantly cleaving to Him by faith. The will of the person must of necessity be ever active. With your will you cleave to Christ or
cleave to something else. It is one thing for you to hold
this special relationship to Christ in theory, and an infinitely different thing to understand it spiritually and to
cleave to Christ in the relation of a constant spiritual outpouring of life from a vine to a branch.[1]

PRAYER

*Dear Father, I thank you for being the Gardener and
planting me where you would have me serve you. I thank
you that your own dear Son Jesus is the Vine, the True
Vine, and that I am one of His branches. I thank you that
I can feel His pulsing life in mine. But it is more than
simply a religion of feeling. I thank you that you have given
me a faith based upon your words. I thank you that I can
read your words in the Bible, and that by my remaining in
your words as true to reality, I can remain in you personally*

---

[1]*Systematic Theology*, pp. 672, 673.

and you can remain in me. Continue to guide me with your written Word and with your hand upon my heart. Plant me and transplant me. Make me to bear fruit wherever I am planted and in all situations. For "this is to by Father's glory, that [I] bear much fruit, showing [myself] to be [Christ's] disciple."[2] Amen.

---

[2]See John 15:8.

26

SHIELD AND REWARD

"After this, the word of the Lord came to Abram in a vision: 'Do not be afraid, Abram. I am your shield, your very great reward'" (Gen. 15:1).

Christ is our Shield. By this name, or in this relation, He has always been known to the saints. God said to Abraham, "I am your shield." Agur realized, "Every word of God is flawless; *he is a shield* to those who take refuge in him. Do not add to his words, or he will rebuke you and prove you a liar" (Prov. 30:5, 6). And David proclaimed, "We wait in hope for the Lord; he is our help and our shield. In him our hearts rejoice, for we trust in his holy name" (Ps. 33:20, 21).

A shield is a piece of defensive armor used in war. It is a broad plate made of metal or wood, and borne upon the arm and hand, and in conflict presented between the body and the enemy to protect it against his arrows or his blows. *God is the Christian's shield in the spiritual warfare.* This is a most interesting and important relation. He who does not know Christ in this relation, and has not embraced and put Him on, as one would buckle on a shield, is exposed to the assaults of the enemy, and will surely be wounded if not slain by his fiery darts. This is more than a figure of speech.

No fact or reality is of more importance to the Christian than to know how to hide himself behind and in Christ in the hour of conflict. Unless the Christian has on his shield and knows how to use it, he will surely fall in battle. When Satan appears, you must present your shield; you must take refuge behind and in Christ, or all will be defeat and disgrace for you. When faith presents Christ as the shield, Satan retires vanquished from the field in every instance. Christ always makes a way for our escape; never did a person get wounded in conflict who made the proper use of Christ his shield. But Christ needs to be known as our protection, ready on all occasions to shield us from the curse of the law and from the artillery of the enemy of our souls. Be sure to truly know Him and put Him on in this relation, and then you may always sing of victory.

The Lord is also the Reward of His people. "I am your shield, your very great reward," God said to Abraham. You need to know and embrace Christ as the reward or portion of your soul, as the condition of abiding in Him. You need to know Him as your exceeding great reward— a present, all-satisfying reward. *Unless we know Christ so as to be satisfied with Him, as all we can ask or desire, we will not abstain from all forbidden sources of enjoyment.* Nothing is more indispensable to holiness and to our entire sanctification than to apprehend the fullness there is in Christ as our reward. When you find in Christ all your desires, and all your wants fully met, when you see in Him all that you can conceive of as excellent and desirable, and that He is your reward, you will remain at rest in peace with Him. You will have little temptation to go after other lovers or other sources of enjoyment. You are full. You have enough. You have an infinitely rich and glorious inheritance. What more can you ask or think? If you understand what it is to have Christ as your reward, you know that He is an infinite reward; a reward that eternity can never exhaust or even diminish in the least degree. Your mind and spirit shall throughout eternity increase in the capacity of enjoying this reward of knowing Jesus personally in all of His manifold relationships. And throughout eternity, your mind will never exhaust the infinite fullness of this Divine Reward.[1]

PRAYER

Lord Jesus, as you were the shield and reward of Abraham, be my shield and reward. Stand between Satan and me and defend me from his attacks through my emotions and my mind. Defend me from physical, mental, or spiritual afflictions that he would inflict upon me, or my loved ones, or the Church. Be my only desire and the only reward I seek, both now and for eternity. Amen.

---

[1]*Systematic Theology*, pp. 676, 677.

27

JESUS MY HOPE

"Paul, an apostle of Christ Jesus by the command of God our Savior and of Christ Jesus our hope" (1 Tim. 1:1).

Christ is our Hope, as the Apostle Paul wrote to Timothy. And he encouraged the Colossians with his letter, saying, "To them God has chosen to make known among the Gentiles the glorious riches of this mystery, which is Christ in you, the hope of glory" (Col. 1:27). Our only rational expectation is from Jesus Christ. Christ in us is our hope of glory. Without Christ in us we have no good or well-grounded hope of glory. Neither Christ in the gospel, Christ on the cross, Christ risen, nor Christ in heaven is our only hope. It is Christ *in* us. Christ actually present, living, and reigning in us as really as He lives and reigns in glory: this is our only well-grounded hope.

If you do not know Christ in this relation, you have no well-grounded hope. You cannot be too certain of Christ being hope in you. You do not truly make Christ your hope if you despair of salvation for yourself or for any other person. You may hope that you are a Christian. You may hope that your sins are forgiven, and that you will be saved. But you can have no hope of glory unless Christ is in you the hope of glory. You cannot too fully understand, or too deeply realize, absolute despair of help and salvation in any other possible way except by Christ in you. Christ in you is knowing and embracing Christ as your hope.

Many seem to have conceived Christ only in His outward relationship as an atoning Savior, or as a risen and ascended Savior. But the indispensable necessity of having Christ within them, ruling in their hearts, and establishing His government over their whole being, is a condition of salvation of which they have never thought. *Christ cannot be truly and savingly their hope any further than He is received into and reigns in their souls.* To hope in merely an outward Christ is to hope in vain. To hope in Christ with the true Christian hope implies:

1. The ripe and spiritual comprehension of our hopeless condition without Him. It implies such an understanding of our sins and our relationship to God, the governor of the universe, as to annihilate all hope of salvation upon legal grounds.

2. Such a perception of our spiritual bondage to sin, as to annihilate all hope of salvation without His constant influence and strength to keep us from sin.

3. Such a knowledge of our circumstances of temptation as to empty us of all expectation of fighting our own battles, or of making the least bit of headway against our spiritual foes in our own wisdom and strength.

4. A complete annihilation of all hope from any other source.

5. The Holy Spirit's revelation of Christ to our souls as our only hope.

6. The apprehension of Him as one to dwell in us, and to be received by faith to the supreme control of our souls.

7. The hearty and joyful reception of Christ in this relation of the hope of glory. We must dethrone self and reject all selfishness. We must enthrone and crown Jesus Christ in our inner man. When Christ is clearly seen to

be the only hope of the soul, and when He is spiritually received in this relationship, we learn habitually and constantly to lean upon Him, to rest in Him, and make no efforts without Him.[1]

PRAYER

Lord Jesus, you indeed are my hope of glory. I ask that you come into my life and take your rightful place upon the throne of my heart. Even as I sing, "Crown Him with many crowns," may I be praying that millions of people will place a crown upon your head and make you king and lord of their individual lives. You are the only hope for the world, especially as you set up your reign within every heart. May people, even now, ask you willingly to be lord of their lives that they may not see you only wielding an iron scepter over them and sealing their fate for eternity by their rejection of you. Amen.

---

[1]*Systematic Theology*, pp. 677, 678.

28

CHRIST MY SALVATION

"Then Moses and the Israelites sang this song to the Lord: 'I will sing to the Lord, for he is highly exalted. The horse and its rider he has hurled into the sea. The Lord is my strength and my song; he has become my salvation'" (Ex. 15:1, 2).

Christ is also our Salvation. As David says, "The Lord is my light and my salvation—whom shall I fear?" (Ps. 27:1). And again, "He alone is my rock and my salvation; he is my fortress, I will not be shaken. My salvation and my honor depend on God; he is my mighty rock, my refuge" (Ps. 62:6, 7). And Isaiah proclaimed, "Surely God is my salvation; I will trust and not be afraid. The Lord, the Lord, is my strength and my song; he has become my salvation" (Isa. 12:2). And again, "It is too small a thing for you to be my servant to restore the tribes of Jacob and bring back those of Israel I have kept. I will also make you a light for the Gentiles, that you may bring my salvation to the ends of the earth" (Isa. 49:6). And when the baby Jesus was placed in the arms of Simeon, he praised God, saying, "Sovereign Lord, as you have promised, you now dismiss your servant in peace. For my eyes have seen your salvation, which you have prepared in the sight of all people, a light for revelation to the Gentiles and for glory to your people Israel" (Luke 2:29–32). These and multitudes of similar passages present Christ, not only as our Savior, but also as our Salvation.

Jesus saves us by becoming himself our Salvation. Becoming our Salvation includes and implies the following:

1. Atonement for our sins.

2. Convincing us of and converting us from our sins.

3. Sanctifying our souls.

4. Justifying, or pardoning and accepting, or receiving us to favor.

5. Giving us eternal life and happiness.

6. The bestowment of himself upon us as the reward of our souls.

7. The everlasting union of our souls with God.

All this Christ is to us; He may well be regarded as not only our Savior, but as our Salvation. Nothing is or can be more important than for us to apprehend Christ in the fullness of His relations to us. Many seem to have extremely superficial experience and knowledge of Christ. They seem in a great measure blind to the length, and breadth, and height, and depth of their infinite needs and necessities. Hence, they have never sought for such a remedy as is found in Christ. The great mass of professing Christians seems to conceive of the salvation of Christ as consisting in a state of mind resulting not from a real union of the soul with Christ, but resulting merely from understanding and believing the doctrines of Christ. The doctrine of Christ, as taught in the Bible, was designed to gain for Christ a personal reception to dwell within and to rule over us. He that truly believes the gospel will receive Christ as He is presented in the gospel; that is, for what He is there asserted to be to His people in all the relations He sustains to our souls, as fast as these relations are revealed to us by the Holy Spirit.

The newly converted person knows Christ in but a few

relations, perhaps only as Christ, Lord, and Savior. The new Christian needs trials and experience to develop his weakness, and to reveal to him his multiplied needs, and thus lead him to a fuller knowledge of Christ. The new convert embraces Christ only so far as he knows Him. At first, he knows little of his need of Him except in His governmental relations. Subsequent experience is a condition of his knowing Christ in all His fullness. Nor can he be effectually taught the fullness there is in Christ any faster than his trials develop his real needs. *If he embraces all he understands of Christ, this is his present duty; but, as trials are in his way, he will learn more of his own necessities. He must learn more of Christ and appropriate Him in new relations, or he will surely fall.*[1]

PRAYER

Dear Heavenly Father, thank you for sending your dear Son to be my Salvation. Not just salvation from hell, but salvation from sin in this life, so I can glorify you now, this is my greatest need. Thank you for meeting my need, and may I show others how you will meet all their needs and necessities through Jesus in all His relations to us. Amen.

---

[1]*Systematic Theology*, pp. 678, 679.

29

CHRIST MY ROCK

"May the words of my mouth and the meditation of my heart be pleasing in your sight, O Lord, my Rock and my Redeemer" (Ps. 19:14).

"To you I call, O Lord my Rock; do not turn a deaf ear to me. For if you remain silent, I will be like those who have gone down to the pit" (Ps. 28:1). Christ is the Rock, and the Rock of our Salvation. As King David prayed to Him, he said, "Turn your ear to me, come quickly to my rescue; be my rock of refuge, a strong fortress to save me. Since you are my rock and my fortress, for the sake of your name lead and guide me" (Ps. 31:2, 3).

It is deeply interesting and moving to contemplate the relations in which Christ revealed himself to the Old Testament saints. He is a rock of salvation, a stronghold or place of refuge. In this relation you must know Him and take hold of Him, or take shelter in Him.

He is the Rock from which the waters of life flow. As the Apostle Paul was inspired to write of Him, "They were all baptized into Moses in the cloud and in the sea. They all ate the same spiritual food and drank the same spiritual drink; for they drank from the spiritual rock that accompanied them, and that rock was Christ" (1 Cor. 10:2–

4). As such, you must know and embrace Him.

Christ is a Great Rock that is higher than we, rising amid the burning sands of our pilgrimage, under the cooling shadow of which the soul can find repose and comfort. He is like the shadow of a great rock in a weary land. To know Christ in this relation, you need to be brought into sharp and protracted trials until you are faint and ready to sink in discouragement. When the struggle is too severe for longer endurance, and you are on the point of giving up in despair, then when Christ is revealed as a great rock standing for our defense against the heat of your trials, and throwing over you the cooling, soothing influence of His protection, you find yourself refreshed and at rest. You readily adopt the language of a numerous class of passages of Scripture and find yourself to have discovered Christ, as inspired men have discovered and embraced Him.

It is truly remarkable, that in all our experiences, we can find that inspired writers have had similar ones to ours. In every trial, and in every deliverance; in every new discovery of our emptiness, and in every discovery of Christ's fullness, we find the language of our hearts most fully and aptly expressed in the language of the living oracles, the Word of God. We readily discover that inspired men have fallen into similar trials, and that Christ has revealed himself to them in the same relationships that He has had with us. The titles and names that they gave Him were revealed to them by Him through their experiences of deliverance in times of trial.

We can appropriate for ourselves these same names of deliverance in our times of trial, and have Him reveal himself personally and savingly to us. We find indeed that the inspired men of the Scriptures had exercises of mind similar to ours in times of trial. Yet, no language of our own can compare and so readily express all that we think, feel, and see, regarding our Rock of Salvation as do their words in the Scriptures.

He is the Rock from which you are satisfied as with honey. "But you would be fed with the finest of wheat; with honey from the rock I would satisfy you" (Ps. 81:16). The spiritual mind grasps this language spiritually, as it is doubtless really intended to be understood. The spiritual mind knows what it is to be satisfied with honey from the Rock, Christ. The divine sweetness that often refreshes the spiritual mind when it partakes of the Rock, Christ, reminds it of the words of this passage of Scripture.

Christ is the Rock or Foundation upon which the Church, as the temple of the Living God, is built. The following makes this clear. "And I tell you that you are Peter, and on this rock I will build my church, and the gates of Hades will not overcome it" (Matt. 16:18), said Jesus, speaking of Peter's confession. And Paul quotes the Old Testament prophet, saying, "See, I lay in Zion a stone that causes men to stumble and a rock that makes them fall, and the one who trusts in him will never be put to shame" (Rom. 9:33). Peter also writes, "Now to you who believe, this stone is precious. But to those who do not believe, 'The stone the builders rejected has become the capstone,' and, 'A stone that causes men to stumble and a rock that makes them fall.' They stumble because they disobey the message—which is also what they were destined for" (1 Pet. 2:7, 8).

Christ is a sure foundation. He is an eternal rock, or the Rock of Ages—the cornerstone of the whole spiritual edifice. But we must build for ourselves upon this rock. It is not enough to understand as a tenet, a theory, an opinion, an article of our creed, that Christ is the rock in this sense. We must see that we do not build upon the sand. "But everyone who hears these words of mine and does not put them into practice is like a foolish man who built his house on sand. The rain came down, the streams rose, and the winds blew and beat against that house, and it fell with a great crash" (Matt. 7:26, 27).[1]

---

[1]*Systematic Theology*, pp. 679, 680.

PRAYER

Dear Heavenly Father, thank you for your Word. Thank you for your Word who created the heavens and the earth. Thank you for your Word who inspired the prophets, the apostles, and the writers of Sacred Scripture. Thank you for your Word who became flesh and dwelt among us, teaching us, modeling life for us, and dying on the cross for us. Thank you for your Word who conquered death and the grave for us, for I know that your Word can never be silenced. Thank you for your written Word, that I may read it, meditate upon it, and take it into my life. Fill me with your Word of truth and with your Holy Spirit that I might proclaim your Word, and the reality of your being our Rock and our Redeemer, a sure shelter in times of trouble and the cornerstone of your people. Amen.

30

STRENGTH OF MY HEART

"God is our refuge and strength, an ever present help in trouble" (Ps. 46:1).

Jesus Christ is the strength of my heart. He is not only our refuge and strength in our conflicts and outward temptations and trials, in the sense expressed in Ps. 46:1, but He is also the strength of our heart and our reward and portion forever, in the sense of Ps. 73:26: "My flesh and my heart may fail, but God is the strength of my heart and my portion forever." He braces up and confirms the whole inner man in the way of holiness. What Christian has not at times found himself ready to halt and faint by the way. Temptation seems to steal upon him like a charm. He finds his spiritual strength very low, his resolution weak, and he feels as if he should give way to the slightest temptation. He is afraid to expose himself out of his closet, or even to remain within it lest he should sin. He says with grief and fear, "I shall fall at the hands of my enemy." He finds himself empty, all weakness and trembling. Were it not that the strength of his heart interposes in time, he would doubtless realize in his experience his worst fears.

But who that knows Christ has not often experienced His faithfulness under such circumstances, and felt an immortal awakening, reviving strength taking possession of his whole being? What spiritual minister has not often dragged himself into the pulpit, so discouraged and faint as to be hardly able to stand, or to hold up his head? He is so weak that his spiritual knees smite one against the other. He is truly empty, and feels as if he could not open his mouth. He sees himself to be an empty vine, an empty vessel, a poor helpless, strengthless infant, lying in the dust before the Lord, unable to stand, or go, or preach, or pray, or do the least thing for Christ. But lo! At this juncture his spiritual strength is renewed. Christ the strength of his heart develops His own almightiness within him. His mouth is open. He is strong in faith, giving glory to God. He is made at once a sharp threshing instrument, to beat down the mountains of opposition to Christ and His gospel. His bow is renewed in his hand and abides in strength. His mouth is opened, and Christ fills it with arguments. Christ has girded him to the battle, and made strong the arms of his hands, with the strength of the mighty God of Jacob.

The same in substance is true of every Christian. He has his seasons of being empty that he may feel his dependence; and shortly he is girded with strength from on high, and an immortal and superhuman strength takes possession of his soul. The enemy gives way before him. In Christ he can run through a troop, and in His strength he can leap over a wall. Every difficulty gives way before him, and he is conscious that Christ has strengthened him with strength in his soul. The will seems to have the utmost decisive power, so that temptation gets an emphatic no! Christ so strengthens us that with evil there is not a moment of parley.[1]

PRAYER

Lord Jesus, strength of my heart, thank you for being all that you are to me. Thank you for taking the time to

---

[1] *Systematic Theology*, pp. 680, 681.

reveal yourself in the multitude of ways we find in the Scriptures; because in all these ways we can find you, our strength to overcome the world, the flesh, and the devil. Thank you for the strength you give each day—especially whenever feelings of hopelessness drive me to you and you so graciously give me the strength to overcome all my trials and temptations. May I continually learn more about who you are personally as I read the Scriptures and apply them to my life. Amen.

31

HOLINESS IN CHRIST

Personal holiness, made possible by the indwelling of Christ himself, is essential to salvation and a creditable Christian witness. It is through Christ that we may reckon ourselves dead indeed to sin and alive to God. We are exhorted and commanded to reckon ourselves dead to sin and alive to God. That is, we may and ought to consider or reckon ourselves, through Him, as dead to sin and alive to God. But what is implied in this liberty to reckon ourselves dead to sin and alive to God through Jesus Christ our Lord? Why certainly that:

1. Through and in Him we have all the provision we need to keep us from sin.

2. We may expect, and ought to expect, to live without sin.

3. We ought to account ourselves as having nothing more to do with sin than a dead man has with the affairs of this world.

4. We may and ought to lay hold on Christ for this full and present death to sin and life unto God.

5. As we do thus reckon ourselves dead to sin and alive to God, in the spiritual sense of this text, we shall find Christ unto our souls all we expect of Him in this relationship of personal holiness. If Christ cannot, or will not,

save us from sin upon condition of our laying hold of Him, and reckoning ourselves dead to sin and alive to God through Him, what right did the Apostle Paul have to say, "Count yourselves dead to sin but alive to God in Christ Jesus" (Rom. 6:11). What! Does the Apostle tell us to count ourselves dead indeed to sin, and shall ministers tell us that such reckoning or expectation is a dangerous delusion?

Now certainly nothing less can be meant by counting ourselves dead to sin and alive to God through Jesus Christ than that through Christ we should expect to live without sin. And not to expect to live without sin through Christ is unbelief. It is a rejection of Christ in this relationship of indwelling Spirit and liberator from the power of sin. Through Christ we ought to expect to live to God as much as we expect to live at all. He who does not expect this rejects Christ as his sanctification and Jesus who saves His people from their sins.

In the previous chapters, I have discussed some of the relations which Christ sustains to us as to our salvation. I could have enlarged greatly, as you perceive, upon each of these, and easily have swelled this study into a large volume. I have only touched upon these relations as specimens of the manner in which He is presented for our acceptance in the Bible and by the Holy Spirit impressed upon our souls. *Do not understand me as teaching that we must first know Christ in all these relations before we can be sanctified.* The thing intended is, that *coming to know Christ in these relations is a condition, or an indispensable means, of our steadfastness or perseverance in holiness under temptation. When we are tempted from time to time, nothing can secure us against a fall but the revelation of Christ to us in these relations one after another, and our appropriation of Him to ourselves by faith. The gospel has directly promised in every temptation to open a way of escape, so that we shall be able to bear it. The spirit of this*

promise pledges to us such a revelation of Christ as to se-
cure our standing if we will lay hold upon Him by faith as
revealed in the Scriptures.

Our circumstances of temptation render it necessary
that at one time we should discover Christ in one relation,
and at another time in another. For example, at one time
we are tempted to despair by Satan's accusing us of sin
and suggesting that our sins are too great to be forgiven.
In this case, we need a revelation and an appropriation of
Christ as having been made sin for us; that is, as having
atoned for our sins—as being our justification or righteousness. This will sustain the soul's confidence and pre-
serve its peace.

At another time we are tempted to despair of ever overcoming our tendencies to sin, and to give up our sanctification as a hopeless thing. Now we need a revelation
of Christ as our sanctification, etc.

At another time the soul is harassed with the view of
the great subtlety and cunning of its spiritual enemies,
and greatly tempted to despair on that account. Now it
needs to know Christ as its wisdom.

Again, it is tempted to discouragement on account of
the great number and strength of its adversaries. On such
occasions it needs Christ revealed as the Mighty God, as
its strong tower, its hiding place, and its arsenal.

Again, the soul is oppressed with a sense of the infinite
holiness of God, and the infinite distance there is between
us and God, on account of our sinfulness and His infinite
holiness, and on account of His infinite abhorrence of sin.
Now the soul needs to know Christ as its righteousness,
and as a mediator between God and man. The soul needs
to know Christ as the surety of a covenant better than the
first, that is, founded on better promises; as an underwri-
ter or endorser of our obligation: as one who undertakes
for us, and pledges himself as our security, to fulfill for
and in us all the conditions of our salvation. To know and

appropriate Christ by faith in this relation is no doubt a condition of our entire sanctification in the sense of continued sanctification.

Again, the Christian's mouth is closed with a sense of guilt so that he cannot look up, nor speak to God of pardon and acceptance. He trembles and is confounded before God. He lies down, on his bed or on the floor, and despairing thoughts roll a tide of agony through his soul. He is speechless, and can only groan out his self-accusations before the Lord. Now as a condition of rising above this temptation to despair, he needs a revelation of Christ as his Advocate, as his High Priest, as ever living to make intercession for him. This view of Christ will enable the soul to commit all to Him in this relation, and maintain its peace and hold on to its sanctification.

Again, the soul is led to tremble in view of its constant exposedness to attacks on every side, oppressed with such a sense of its own utter helplessness in the presence of its enemies, as almost to despair. Now it needs to know Christ as the Good Shepherd, who keeps a constant watch over the sheep and carries the lambs in His bosom. The soul needs to know Him as a watchman and a keeper.

Again, we can be oppressed with a sense of our own utter emptiness, and are forced to exclaim, "I know that in me (that is, in my flesh,) dwelleth no good thing" (Rom. 7:18, KJV). We see that we have no life, or unction, or power, or spirituality within ourselves. Now we need to know Christ as the True Vine from which we may receive constant and abundant spiritual nourishment. We need to know Him as the fountain of the water of life, and in those relations that will meet our necessities in this direction. These examples illustrate that entire or permanent sanctification depends on the continuing revelation and appropriation of Christ in the fullness of His various official relationships.

I do not intend, as I have said, that Christ must be

previously known in all these relations before a soul can be sanctified at all; but that, when tested from time to time, a new revelation of Christ to the soul, corresponding to the temptation, is a condition of remaining steadfast in personal holiness. This gracious aid or revelation is abundantly promised in the Bible, and will be made in time, so that by laying hold of holiness in Christ in the present revealed relation, you may be preserved blameless, though the furnace of temptation be heated seven times better than it needs to be.

In my estimation, the church as a body—I mean the nominal church—has entirely mistaken the nature and means (conditions) of sanctification. They have not regarded it as consisting in a state of entire consecration, have not understood that continual entire consecration is entire sanctification. *They have regarded sanctification as consisting in the annihilation of the constitutional propensities (natural desires or inclinations), instead of the controlling of them. They have erred equally in regard to the means or conditions of entire sanctification. They seem to regard sanctification as brought about by a physical cleansing in which man is passive; or to go over to the opposite extreme, and regard sanctification as consisting in the formation of habits of obedience.*

The old school (Calvinists) seem to be waiting for a physical sanctification in which they are to be mainly passive, and which they do not expect to take place in this life. Holding as they do, that the constitution of both soul and body is defiled or sinful in every power and faculty, they of course cannot hold to entire sanctification in this life. If the constitutional appetites, passions, and propensities (natural desires or inclinations) are in fact, as they hold, sinful in themselves, then the question is settled: entire sanctification cannot take place in this world, nor in the next, unless the constitution be radically changed, and that of course by the creative power of God.

The new school (Calvinists), rejecting the doctrine of constitutional moral depravity, and physical regeneration and sanctification, have lost sight of Christ as our sanctification. They have fallen into a self-righteous view of sanctification and hold that sanctification is effected by works, or by forming holy habits. Both the old and the new school (Calvinists) have fallen into grave errors upon this fundamentally important subject.

The truth is, beyond all question, that sanctification is by faith as opposed to works.[1] That is, faith receives Christ in all His offices; and in all the fullness of His relations to our souls. And Christ, when received, works in our souls to will and to do all His good pleasure, not by a physical, but by a moral or persuasive working. Observe, He influences the will. This must be by a moral influence if the will's actings are intelligent and free, as they must be to be holy. That is, if He influences the will to obey God, it must be by a divine moral persuasion. The soul never in any instance obeys in a spiritual and true sense unless it is influenced by the indwelling Spirit of Christ. But whenever Christ is discovered and received in any relation, in that relation you are full and perfect, so that we are complete in Him. For it has pleased the Father that in Christ all the fullness of God should dwell, and that we should all receive of His fullness until we have grown up in Him in all things.[2]

---

[1]See especially, Finney's sermons, "Sanctification by Faith," in *Principles of Victory*, pp. 46–54; and "Sanctification Under Grace," in *Principles of Liberty*, pp. 55–64; and both "Putting on Christ" and "Fullness There Is in Christ," in *Principles of Holiness*, pp. 124–134, 168–179.
[2]*Systematic Theology*, pp. 681, 682, 683, 638, 639, 684.

Appendix 1:

HOLINESS ESSENTIAL TO SALVATION.*

A Sermon preached on Friday, June 7, 1850, by the Rev. C. G. Finney, of the Oberlin Collegiate Institute, America, at the Tabernacle, Moorfields (Whitefield's Tabernacle).

"She will give birth to a son, and you are to give him the name Jesus, because he will save his people from their sins" (Matt. 1:21).

In speaking from these words, I design to show:

    I. That salvation from sin is the great necessity of man.
   II. That Jesus has undertaken this work.
 III. Inquire why it is that so many persons fail of this salvation.

I. *That salvation from sin is the great necessity of man.* This is a fact of universal observation. It is also a fact of universal consciousness. Every man is conscious of the fact that he is a sinner, and while he is a sinner he cannot

---

*No. 1,566 from *The Penny Pulpit.*

be satisfied with himself, he cannot truly respect himself, he cannot have peace of mind, he cannot have the favor of God; and he ought not to have all or any of these things. In short, it is a fact of universal experience that men are sinners, and that they must be saved from sin as a condition of their being made happy, either in this world or in the future world. Men are so constituted that they know unquestionably that ultimate happiness is impossible unless they can be delivered from that which they know to be a great curse in this world, and which they also know will be their ultimate ruin, if persisted in. Men know that happiness is impossible while they are violating their own consciences. These facts are always assumed in the Bible, and their truth is declared by the universal sentiment of mankind. But I must not dwell on this thought; the text announces the fact that Jesus Christ has come into the world, and that His great business is to save men from sin. This leads me to the second thought.

II. *That Jesus has undertaken this work.* "He will save his people from their sins" (Matt. 1:21). Therefore is His name called Jesus—the name *Jesus* signifying a Savior. Now, salvation from sin is of the highest importance to mankind. The term strictly, as here used, means merely deliverance, or safety from some tremendous evil. It is often found in the Bible, and includes in it very generally, in addition to mere deliverance, the result of it—eternal happiness and enjoyment in heaven with the people of God. Thus, properly and scripturally speaking, the term salvation means deliverance, both from guilt and its consequences. In this text, the reason assigned for the name that was to be given to the child of Mary was that He should save his people from their sins—that He should bear the particular relation of a Savior—that He should save both from the guilt and the punishment of sin. The Bible represents Him as having given himself to be the Savior of the world, as having consecrated himself to this end, as having died and opened a way by which sinners could be saved. Previous to this, as being in a waiting attitude to accomplish this work; as endeavoring to gain the consent of God and man to comply with the natural and necessary conditions of sinners being saved; and that now He possesses in himself all the fullness of power necessary to the accomplishment of the work—He is able to save unto the uttermost all that will come to God by Him. The Bible represents Jesus as coming on this great mission, and as occupying himself exclusively with this work, and as having fully secured this end. Now, whenever persons come into sympathy with Him, and seek what is His business to give, knock at the door which is His business to open, the Bible represents Him as ready and willing to do these things for them. We now come to the third inquiry.

III. *Why it is that so many persons fail of this salvation.* That many do fail is a simple matter of fact. Now, the question is, *Why do they fail?* We remark, first, that many persons fail of this salvation because they have not abandoned reliance upon themselves. It is the most obvious thing in the whole world that many persons are living not to God but to themselves. Now, wherever this principle is manifested, it is certain that persons are not saved from sin, for what is sin but living to self and not to God. Self-seeking is the very essence of sin. Now, multitudes of persons manifest that this spirit is not set aside in them, but that, on the contrary, the whole end and aim of their life is self-seeking, instead of the first and great end being the glory and honor of God. Now, a man cannot be saved unless he is justified, and he cannot be justified unless his sins are pardoned—this must be a condition of a sinner's salvation. Salvation consists in being saved *from* sin; and the reason why a great many persons are not saved is that they are unwilling to accept salvation on such a condition—they are unwilling to give up their sins. But if they will not be persuaded to be saved from their sins, and become sanctified, if they will not relinquish and renounce their sin, they never can be saved. Many persons will even pray to God that He will save them, but they really do not desire that for which they ask—they do not mean what they say. To get men to consent to relinquish their sins is the great difficulty. Now observe, if a man is saved at all he must consent to it, his will must acquiesce in the arrangement; and the will is not moved by physical force. A man must voluntarily consent to be saved, or Jesus himself cannot possibly save him. Man is a moral agent, and he is addressed by God as such; therefore, in order to be saved, he must voluntarily consent to relinquish sin, and have his mind brought into obedience with the law of God.

Again: Multitudes are not saved because they seek forgiveness while they do not forsake their sins. Some individuals will spend much time in praying for pardon while they indulge themselves in sin. Again: Multitudes are seeking for salvation while they neglect the natural condition of their being pardoned. While they continue in sin, indulging in a self-seeking spirit, it is naturally impossible that they can be saved. If a man should indulge in relation to his body, everyone would plainly perceive the folly of his conduct. If he should partake of things which rendered good health impossible, and yet should wonder that he did not possess the robust health which he desired, people would not pity, but blame him. Now, the fact is, that many persons are seeking for that which must result alone from holiness while they are not themselves sanctified. They are seeking comfort while they refuse to be holy; thus they neglect to fulfill the natural conditions on which either comfort or salvation can be obtained.

Again, many persons fail of this salvation because they are waiting for God to fulfill conditions which it is naturally impossible for Him to fulfill, and which they themselves must fulfill, and which God is endeavoring to persuade and influence them to fulfill! For example, God cannot repent for them; He cannot believe for them; no, but these are the natural conditions of their salvation, and these very things Christ is persuading them to do. Now, they are waiting for God to do that which He will never do, that, in fact, which He cannot do, but which He is requiring us to do for ourselves. Let me be understood. God never requires of us to perform an impossibility, nor does He accomplish that for us which we can do ourselves. Don't be shocked at this, for it is truth. Now, observe, God requires us to repent; this is an act of our own minds, and therefore He cannot do it for us. It is true that these things are spoken of sometimes as being done by God. It is said that He gives repentance, faith, and love, but He only does this in the sense of persuading and inciting our minds to the performance of these duties. Now, if anybody is seeking for God to do that which they must do themselves, they will fail of eternal life. How many are making mistakes in this matter! They are waiting for God to put repentance and faith into them, and entirely overlooking the fact of its being an exercise of their own minds.

Again, another difficulty, and another reason, why persons are not saved is this—they profess to be waiting for the Holy Spirit, while in fact they are resisting the Holy Spirit. They pretend that they are waiting for the Holy Spirit to save them and convert them; but every moment they wait, they are grieving and resisting the Holy Spirit. Now, what do they mean by waiting when they ought to be acting? From the beginning and end He is the teacher. "No one can come to me unless the Father who sent me draws him" (John 6:44). "They will all be taught by God" (John 6:45). "The Spirit will take from what is mine and make it known to you" (John 16:15). Now, the Bible represents the Holy Spirit in this way as a teacher, and those who do not yield when the truth is presented to them are resisting and grieving the Spirit. You remember the words of Stephen to the Jews: "You are just like your fathers: You always resist the Holy Spirit" (Acts 7:51). Now, multitudes in the present day are resisting the Holy Spirit under the pretense of waiting for Him. The divine influence is always waiting to save you if you will comply with the necessary conditions; but if under any pretense you neglect your duty, you never will be saved. But I pass next to consider another great difficulty in the way of a sinner's conversion.

Many are really seeking to be justified *in* sin. They ask God to pardon them, but they refuse to be sanctified; they seek Christ as their justification only. They cleave to their sins, they are living in their sins, and they seek to be justified rather than sanctified—indeed, they refuse to be sanctified at all. Now, this is a very common case. Again, let me say that this class of persons really regard the gospel as a mighty system of indulgence, on a large scale. They really suppose that men are subjects of this salvation while they are living in selfish indulgence. In the very early ages of Christianity, the Antinomian spirit had crept into the church: the doctrine of justification by faith as opposed to justification by works was sadly abused by many. While some of the Apostles were still living, many persons came to regard the gospel as a system of indulgence, that men were to be justified *in* sin rather than be saved *from* sin; thus they took an entirely false view of the gospel of Christ. You will remember that the Apostle James wrote his epistle to denounce this wrong view, and to guard the Christians against abusing the doctrine of justification by faith. Some persons imagine that the Apostle rejected this doctrine altogether, yet this is not true. But his epistle being written for the purpose we have mentioned, he does not give this doctrine the prominence that Paul did. Now, no man who lives in sin can be justified, because no man can be pardoned who lives in any form of iniquity. The Apostle tells you plainly that those who commit sin are the children of the devil, and while they are *living in sin* they cannot enjoy the privileges of the gospel. He does not mean that an individual cannot be a Christian who falls under the power of temptation and into occasional sin. The Apostle John also says, "Anyone born of God does not continue to sin" (1 John 5:18). "No one who is born of God will continue to sin, because God's seed remains in him; he cannot go on sinning because he has been born of God" (1 John 3:9). "He who does what is sinful is of the devil" (1 John 3:8). This is strong language, and if I should affirm so strongly the necessity of holiness, you would think I spoke harshly; but it ought to be insisted upon more than it is, that men cannot be Christians unless they are holy. The moral law is as much binding upon Christians as it was upon those to whom it was first given. Faith without love will never save man; but let me say that true faith is always true love. Every man who breaks the law systematically and designedly, living in violation of its precepts, is a child of the devil and not of God. Let this be thundered in the ears of the church and the world. Now, it is very common for men to overlook this great truth, and fall into the worldly-mindedness and sinful practices of those around them.

Again multitudes are not saved because they regard the gospel as an abrogation of the moral law—a virtual repeal of it. Now, the gospel does not repeal the moral law. What does the Apostle say, "Do we, then, nullify the law by this faith? Not at all! Rather, we uphold the law" (Rom. 3:31). Now, it is true that the gospel was designed to set aside the penalty of the law upon all who should be persuaded to come back to its precepts, and yield that love and confidence which the law requires. Now, it is frequently the case, if ministers begin to say anything about obedience to the law, the people call out against it as legal preaching! If they are roused up and urged to do that which the law of God requires of them, they tell you they want the gospel. Now, such people know nothing at all of the gospel! They make Christ the minister of sin! They seem to think that Christ came to justify them in their sin instead of saving them from it.

Let me say once more, that another reason why men are not saved from sin is that they have really come to regard justification in sin as a means to save them from it! In support of this monstrous idea, they will even appeal to the Scriptures. They found justification in the atonement; now, this work of Christ can never be imputed to any man in such a sense as to justify him while he remains in sin! Justification *in* sin is a thing impossible! Now, how can a man be pardoned and justified before he repents and believes! It is impossible! He must be in a state of obedience to the law of God before he can be justified! The fact is, there is a very great mistake among many people on this subject. They think that they must persuade themselves that they are justified, but they are not, and never can be, till they forsake sin and do their duty. In the next place, multitudes make this mistake—they seek hope, rather than holiness; instead of working out their own salvation, they seek to cherish a hope that they shall be saved. Again, they seek to persuade themselves that they are safe, while they are in a state of condemnation. Those who seek salvation ofttimes fail because they seek it selfishly; not so much because they abhor sin, and want holiness, as because they desire personal happiness, or personal honor, by being held up as very pure and good men; and because they seek sanctification for some selfish reason they do not get rid of their sins. Again, some individuals content themselves in sin so long as they can indulge a hope, or get others to indulge a hope for them. If they have certain feelings, which lead them to hope that all will be well with them at last, they are perfectly satisfied and have no desire to be saved from sin.

REMARKS

But I cannot continue this train of observation, and will therefore conclude with some remarks. First, no person has any right to hope for eternal life unless he is conscious of possessing the spirit of Christ within him—unless he is free from those sinful tempers which are indulged in by wicked men; unless he is free from a self-seeking spirit of doing business which characterizes the men of the world. How can a man in such a condition expect or hope for eternal life? How can any man suppose that he is justified before he is sanctified? I do not mean to say that a man is not in any sense justified before he is sanctified; but, as a matter of fact, a man is not safe for eternity unless he is saved from sin. *He has no right to expect to get to heaven unless the work of sanctification is going on in his soul.*

Again, it is easy to see from what has been said, that many persons regard the doctrine of justification by faith as the whole gospel. It is the gospel, in their conception of it. Now, why is this the gospel to them? Why is it good news? Why is it not good news that Christ will save them from sin? How is it that the good news of the gospel as it strikes them is the good news that will justify rather than sanctify?—that Christ is precious to them, not so much because He came to save from sin, as because He came to forgive, to die for their sins, and to justify them? Is there not something wrong in all this? Does it not show, when persons lay more stress upon justification than upon sanctification that they are more afraid of punishment than of sin? More afraid of the consequences of sin than of the sin itself? If they can but get rid of the penalty, the governmental consequence of sin, they are satisfied.

Again, it is certain that where this principle takes possession of the mind, the individual seeks much more to be pardoned than to be made holy. It is better news to him that Christ will justify him than that Christ will save him from his sins. Talk to him about his sins; preach to him about his sins; require him to become holy; present Christ as his sanctification, and that is not the gospel! Let me say, there are multitudes of persons who have contracted their views into that one point—that Christ has died to save men from punishment. All idea about Christ being the believer's sanctification, or that sanctification is a condition of salvation, is wholly lost sight of. There is no stress laid upon the doctrine of sanctification. Christ is chiefly precious because He saves from wrath, much more than because He saves from sin; more because He justifies than because He sanctifies. Now, rely upon it, that, whenever this is the case, there is a sad defect of character. What is the true spirit of the children of God? Why, it is this, they feel as if they must get rid of sin, at any rate. They don't want to be saved in their sins; they feel that to live in their sins is hell enough. They abhor themselves on account of their sins. They must get away from their sins. They would not wish to be saved at all if they could not be saved from sin. They are ready to say, "If the gospel cannot save me from sin, it is a failure, for this is my necessity." Now, who does not know that the true Christian is more afraid of sin than of punishment? Yes, and a great deal more! They abhor sin; and when they ever fall into sin, they are ready to curse themselves; and all the more because Christ is so willing to forgive them. The man in this condition of mind will never look upon the gospel as mere justification.

Again, whenever the doctrine of justification comes to be more prominent in the church than sanctification, there is something wrong, there is a radical error crept into the church; there is a danger of that church losing all true idea of what the gospel is. I don't know how it is in this country, but I greatly fear that the doctrine of sanctification is kept very much in the background. Now, why is this? While there is so much said about justification, there is very little said about personal holiness. So much is said about a Savior, as if the gospel was meant simply to save men from punishment. Now, while I know that the gospel presents salvation from punishment, and the promise of eternal life through Jesus Christ, I know that its chief relation to men is to save them from their sins—to become their sanctification.

Again, the true state of men is always known by the great absorbing ideas which are in their minds. A man's character is as the end for which he lives. Now, a man who lives in any sin, any form of self-pleasing and self-seeking, cannot be a Christian; for the true idea of the gospel is, that for a man to be a Christian he must be devoted to God and thoroughly withdrawn from all forms of sin and iniquity. He must be devoted to God, living for God, living for the same end that God lives; sympathizing with Christ and with everything that is good. This is the character of every true Christian. This is the true conception of Christianity; and just in proportion as individuals approach to this standard, they have a good hope of salvation, and just in proportion as they recede from this standard, they fail of salvation.

Again, there are a great many persons whose aim is to get peace of mind, and who are constantly crying "peace" to others when there is no peace. Now, let me say that there can be no real, true peace unless all the conditions of the gospel have been complied with. You cannot have the peace of God which passes all understanding while you are in an unsanctified state; and, if you think so, you are deceiving yourself. Now, let me ask you, "Are you conscious that this peace of God does 'rule in your hearts'?" There are many persons who have been trying for years to make themselves happy, but who, after all, are in such a state of mind as not to know that they are pardoned, have no real confidence in their own piety; now, how is it possible that they should have peace of mind?* Peace of mind results from sanctification, and this they have never obtained. Let an individual who has been making justification the great idea be at the point of death, and does he feel happy and resigned, having a full confidence that he shall go to heaven? How often do we hear such persons exclaim under such circumstances, "I am undone! I am not prepared!" Why are you not prepared? A short time ago you were indulging a comfortable hope that you were a Christian, and now you cry out in fear, lest you should lose your soul. How is this? There is a great delusion in the minds of men on this subject. They suppose that they have a very comfortable hope, but it is in the absence of piety; and when death stares them in the face, they discover that they have no confidence in religion, or any ground of hope.

Again, persons who do not like to have their hopes tried, and themselves searched, do great wrong to their own souls. The more hope is tried, if it be good hope, the more consoling and satisfactory will it become. The man who is seeking to be sanctified desires to be searched that he may not be resting in any degree upon an uncertain and unsafe foundation, because he is more afraid of sin than of anything else. He is more ready to forsake sin than anything else in the world. He would rather forego any earthly good than have anything to do with sin. Now, don't say that this is extreme, because it is a universal truth if religion implies supreme love to God. If we supremely love any being, we shall supremely delight to please him: this is a universal characteristic of the children of God. Now, if this be so, what shall we say of the great mass of professors who give the highest possible evidence that self-indulgence is the chief end of their lives? They wait to be

---

*See especially, "The Kingdom of God in Consciousness," by Charles Finney in *Principles of Liberty*, pp. 183–194.

saved, not from sin, but in it. But while they live in sin they never can be saved! Before hope can be cherished, the conditions of salvation must be fulfilled: you will never be saved at all unless you are saved *from sin*—mind that! You must become holy in order to become happy. Fulfill the conditions; become holy, and then your peace shall flow like a river. Give up your sins, give your heart to God, and rely upon it that the peace which passes all understanding shall rule in your hearts.

Believer in Christ, the Lord hath set you apart for himself, separated you from the rest of the world. You are set apart as *"holy to the Lord"* (Ex. 28:36): this must be written plainly upon you. And if the Lord has written His Name upon you, you are safe. And let me say to everyone, don't you expect to be forgiven, don't you expect to be pardoned, unless you will consent to be separated from your sins, and have the Name of the Lord Jesus Christ written upon your hearts: unless your prayer is, "O Lord, write thy law upon my heart and make me holy." Receive His Name in your forehead and His law in your heart. Give yourself up to him, body and soul, and rely upon it, as the Lord liveth, as Jesus liveth, you shall understand what is the salvation of God. Will you do it? *

---

*For more of Finney's sermons and lectures on Holiness and Sanctification see *Principles of Holiness, Principles of Victory, Principles of Liberty*, and *The Promise of the Spirit*, published by Bethany House Publishers.

APPENDIX 2:

THE NATURE AND NAMES OF CHRIST

To learn more of Jesus Christ personally, Charles G. Finney prayed through the Scriptures; especially those that related to the nature and names of Jesus. He asked the Holy Spirit to reveal Christ to him personally in the relationships that Christ can have with the believer according to His nature and names. The meditations in this book are the result of Finney's serious search for Christ in the Scriptures. Finney encouraged his readers to make a similar attempt to know Christ in all of His relations as the only Way to personal holiness or entire sanctification, in the sense of continual obedience and holiness before God in Jesus Christ through faith in Him. This appendix lists the scripture verses that refer to Christ's nature and name. It is not exhaustive in the sense of including every verse, but a great help in using a concordance to prayerfully consider each verse that refers to each name of Christ. I encourage you to carefully consider and pray over each verse listed here, and ask God to reveal His Son to you personally in each relationship that is described. And I do suggest that you use a concordance with this list, and a good Bible dictionary, such as, *Today's Dictionary of the Bible* (Minneapolis: Bethany House Publishers, 1982), to make an indepth study of who Jesus Christ is. Again, Finney would remind us that this study is not to be just theoretical, but we are to pray for the spiritual meaning of each passage to be impressed by the Holy Spirit upon our mind, emotions, and will.

The following material is taken from the Biblical Cyclopedic Index, The Open Bible Edition—New American Standard Version. Copyright © 1976, 1978 by Thomas Nelson Publishers, pages 88–90. I thank them for their permission to use this material.

Pre-existence of:

Affirmed in Old
 Testament. . . . . .Ps. 2:7
Confirmed by
 Christ . . . . John 8:58
Proclaimed by
 apostles. . . . . . Col. 1:15–19

Birth of:

Predicted . . . . Isa. 7:14
Fulfilled . . . . . . Matt. 1:18–25
In the fullness
 of time . . . . .Gal. 4:4

Deity of:

Prophecy. . . . . Isa. 9:6
Acknowledged by
 Christ . . . . . .John 20:28, 29
Acclaimed by
 witnesses. . . . .John 1:14, 18
Affirmed by
 apostles. . Rom. 9:5; Heb. 1:8

Attributes of:

All-powerful . . . . . Matt. 28:18
All-knowing . . . . Col. 2:3
Ever-present . . . . . Matt. 18:20
Eternal. . . . . . .John 1:1, 2, 15

Humanity of:

Foretold
 . . Gen. 3:15; 1 Cor. 15:45–47

Took man's nature
 . . . . .John 1:14; Heb. 2:9–18
Seed of woman . . . . . .Gal. 4:4
A son of man. . . . . . Luke 3:38
Of David's line . . . Matt. 22:45
A man . . . . 1 Tim. 2:5
Four brothers . . . . . .Mark 6:3

Mission of:

Do God's will. . . . . . John 6:38
Save sinners . . . . . Luke 19:10
Bring in everlasting
 righteousness . . . Dan. 9:24
Destroy Satan's works
 . . . . . Heb. 2:14; 1 John 3:8
Fulfill the Old
 Testament. . . . . .Matt. 5:17
Give life . . . . . .John 10:10, 28
Abolish
 ceremonialism. . . Dan. 9:27
Complete revelation   Heb. 1:1

Worship of, by:

Old Testament
 saints . . . . . . Josh. 5:13–15
Demons. . . . . .Mark 5:6
Men . . . . John 9:38
Angels . . . . Heb. 1:6
Disciples. . . . . Luke 24:52
Saints in glory . . . Rev. 7:9, 10
All . . . . .Phil. 2:10, 11

Character of:

Holy . . . . Luke 1:35
Righteous . . . . Isa. 53:11
Just . . . . Zech. 9:9
Guileless. . . . . 1 Pet. 2:22
Sinless . . . . 2 Cor. 5:21
Spotless . . . . 1 Pet. 1:19
Innocent . . . . Matt. 27:4
Gentle . . . . Matt. 11:29
Merciful . . . . Heb. 2:17
Humble. . . . . Phil. 2:8
Forgiving . . . . 'Luke 23:34

Types of:

Adam . . . . Rom. 5:14
Abel . . . . Heb. 12:24
Moses . . . . Deut. 18:15
Passover . . . . 1 Cor. 5:7
Manna . . . . John 6:32
Brazen serpent . . . . John 3:14

Other names for:

Adam,
    the second . . 1 Cor. 15:45–47
Advocate. . . . . 1 John 2:1
Almighty . . . . Rev. 19:15
Alpha and Omega . . . Rev. 21:6
Amen . . . . Rev. 3:14
Ancient of Days. . . . . Dan. 7:9
Angel of His
    presence . . . . Isa. 63:9
Anointed above His
    fellows. . . . . Ps. 45:7
Anointed of the Lord . . . Ps. 2:2
Apostle of our
    confession . . . . Heb. 3:1
Arm of the Lord . . Isa. 51:9, 10
Author and perfecter of our
    faith . . . . Heb. 12:2
Author of
    salvation . . . . Heb. 2:10
Baby. . . . . Luke 2:16
Beginning and end . . Rev. 21:6
Beloved. . . . . Eph. 1:6
Beloved of God . . . Matt. 12:18
Beloved Son . . . . . . Mark 1:11

Blessed and only
    Sovereign . . . . . 1 Tim. 6:15
Born of God. . . . . . 1 John 5:18
Branch . . . . Zech. 3:8
Branch,
    a righteous . . . . . . Jer. 23:5
Branch of
    righteousness . . . Jer. 33:15
Bread . . . . John 6:41
Bread of Life . . . . . . John 6:35
Bridegroom. . . . . . . John 3:29
Bright morning
    star. . . . . Rev. 22:16
Carpenter . . . . Mark 6:3
Carpenter's son . . . Matt. 13:55
Chief cornerstone
    . . . . Ps. 118:22; Mark 12:10
Chief Shepherd . . . . .1 Pet. 5:4
Child . . . . Isa. 9:6
Child Jesus . . . . Luke 2:27
Choice of God . . . . . .1 Pet. 2:4
Christ, the
    . . . . . John 1:41; Acts 9:22
Christ a King . . . . . Luke 23:2
Christ, Jesus . . . . Rom. 8:2
Christ Jesus
    our Lord . . . . Rom. 8:39
Christ
    of God, the. . . . . . Luke 9:20
Christ, of God, His
    Chosen One. . . . Luke 23:35
Christ, the Lord . . . Luke 2:11
Christ, the
    power of God . . . 1 Cor. 1:24
Christ, the Son
    of the Blessed . . Mark 14:61
Commander . . . . Isa. 55:4
Consolation of
    Israel . . . . Luke 2:25
Costly cornerstone. . Isa. 28:16
Counselor . . . . Isa. 9:6
Covenant of
    the people . . . . . . Isa. 42:6
Deity . . . . Col. 2:9
Deliverer . . . . Rom. 11:26
Diadem. . . . . Isa. 28:5
Door . . . . John 10:2
Door into
    the sheep. . . . . . . John 10:1

Lord Christ . . . . Col. 3:24
Lord God Almighty . . .Rev. 4:8
Lord Jesus . . . . . . .Acts 19:17
Lord Jesus
  Christ . . . . .2 Thess. 2:1
Lord and Savior
  Jesus Christ . . . .2 Pet. 2:20
Lord both of dead
  and living . . . . . . Rom. 14:9
Lord of
  all. . .Acts 10:36; Rom. 10:12
Lord of glory . . . . . . 1 Cor. 2:8
Lord of hosts . . . . Isa. 54:5
Lord of lords . . . . . 1 Tim. 6:15
Lord of Sabbath. . . . . Luke 6:5
Lord our
  righteousness . . . . Jer. 23:6
Lord, your
  redeemer . . . . Isa. 43:14
Majestic One,
  the Lord . . . . Isa. 33:21
Man of peace . . . . . . Luke 10:6
Man of sorrows . . . . . Isa. 53:3
Mediator . . . . .Heb. 12:24
Messenger of
  the covenant . . . . . Mal. 3:1
Messiah . . . . . . .John 4:25, 26
Mighty God . . . . Isa. 9:6
Mighty One
  of Jacob. . . . . Isa. 60:16
Minister of
  the sanctuary . . .Heb. 8:1, 2
Morning star . . . . . .2 Pet. 1:19
Most Mighty . . . . .Ps. 45:3
Nazarene . . . . Matt. 2:23
Offspring of David . . John 7:42
Only begotten of
  the Father . . . . . . John 1:14
Only begotten God. . John 1:18
Only wise God. . . . 1 Tim. 1:17
Our Passover . . . . . 1 Cor. 5:7
Our peace . . . . Eph. 2:14
Physician . . . . Luke 4:23
Power of God. . . . . 1 Cor. 1:24
Precious
  cornerstone . . . . . .1 Pet. 2:6
Priest . . . . Heb. 5:6
Prince. . . . . .Acts 5:31

Prince of life . . . . . . .Acts 3:15
Prince of peace . . . . . . Isa. 9:6
Prophet. . . . . . Deut. 18:15, 18
Propitiation . . . . . . Rom. 3:25
Purifier and refiner . . Mal. 3:3
Rabbi . . . . John 6:25
Rabboni . . . . John 20:16
Ransom. . . . . 1 Tim. 2:6
Redeemer . . . . Isa. 59:20
Resurrection and
  the life . . . . John 11:25
Righteous Judge . . . 2 Tim. 4:8
Righteous man . . . Matt. 27:19
Righteous One . . . . Isa. 53:11
Rock. . . . . 1 Cor. 10:4
Rock of offense . . . . Rom. 9:33
Rod of the stem
  of Jesse . . . . Isa. 11:1
Root of David . . . . .Rev. 22:16
Root of Jesse . . . . . . Isa. 11:10
Rose of Sharon . . . . . Song 2:1
Ruler . . . . .Matt. 2:6
Ruler in Israel. . . . . .Mic. 5:2
Ruler of the kings
  of earth . . . . .Rev. 1:5
Salvation . . . . Luke 2:30
Savior. . . . . 1 Tim. 4:10
Savior,
  Jesus Christ . . . .2 Pet. 2:20
Savior, God our . . . . . Titus 1:3
Savior of
  the world. . . . . . 1 John 4:14
Scepter out
  of Israel. . . . . . . Num. 24:17
Second man. . . . . .1 Cor. 15:47
Seed of the woman. . Gen. 3:15
Servant of the
  circumcision . . . . Rom. 15:8
Shepherd . . . . John 10:11
Shepherd of
  souls . . . . .1 Pet. 2:25
Shoot of the stem of
  Jesse. . . . . Isa. 11:1
Signal of the
  people . . . . Isa. 11:10
Son of
  the Blessed . . . . Mark 14:61
Son of David . . . . . . Matt. 9:27

INDEX TO SCRIPTURE QUOTATIONS